Suburbia's Coddled Kids

SUBURBIA'S
CODDLED
KIDS

PETER
WYDEN

Drawings by F. B. Modell

1962 DOUBLEDAY & COMPANY, INC., GARDEN CITY, N.Y.

For Ronnie and Jeff

Contents

Author's Affidavit

Of all the people across our rich, rolling land, none feel more misunderstood than suburbanites, especially suburban parents. More misunderstood or more maligned. There are, as we shall see, excellent reasons for this sensitivity. I feel impelled, therefore, at the outset of our journey into Suburbia's kindergartens, bowling alleys, police stations, high schools, split-level recreation rooms, psychiatrists' couches, front lawns, back fences, car pools, and kiddie pools, to make certain sworn statements.

These are:

I do not hate suburbs.

I do not believe that the suburban environment of itself induces alcoholism, excessive permissiveness, psycho-pathology (sexual or otherwise), snobbery, delinquency, common colds, or any other failing whatsoever.

I do not believe that the nation's cause would be

advanced by declaring either children or suburbs un-constitutional.

I do not believe that suburbs are, relatively speaking, undesirable settings for rearing children.

I plead guilty of most—if not all—charges raised in the ensuing pages against suburban parents.

I doubt that today's suburban adolescents will, in adulthood, turn out to be any more maladjusted than their forebears.

They will, however, find new ways to be miserable. For I do believe that Suburbia, as we are only now beginning to discern it, has produced a novel and quite unprecedented way of life; that in this restless Utopia a new breed of youngsters is growing up—soon to descend by the millions upon its cars, commuter trains, and automated kitchens to take over from the rest of us; and that these children are endowed with new and remarkable tribal characteristics which have heretofore been but dimly seen.

Of these I sing.

1. The Subdivision Generation

It all began to register with me one sunny Sunday afternoon near the North Shore Railroad tracks in Highland Park, Illinois. I had my two boys aged ten and eight with me, and we were doing something quite extraordinary. We were walking. Even more notable for week-ending suburbanites, we were walking without a plan, without a particular destination, without a deadline when we would have to be some place else. Trudging through a small industrial slum, we came upon a tumble-down residence. We had been past the area many times before—by car, of course—but had never noticed that people lived there. Now we had evidently become curiosities because a small boy peered out of an unpainted door to look us over. He was filthy and shabbily dressed.

"Look, Daddy," said my ten-year-old, "a frontier kid!"

We had not then been living long in Highland Park, a pleasant community near Chicago, but it had quickly become apparent that it was not very different from our previous home towns: Bethesda and Chevy Chase, Maryland, near Washington, D.C., and University City,

Missouri, near St. Louis. I have friends in all these agreeable places. Most of them spend much of their socializing time talking about their children. With considerable regularity, an unsettling theme recurs in these conversations. To wit, what sort of picture of the world are our children getting by growing up in the suburbs? Aren't we all making things much too easy for them? Would they be equipped later to take the knocks of adult existence?

I suspect that the same questions are being ventilated more and more frequently at cocktail parties from Westport, Connecticut, to Santa Monica, California. I also have reason to believe that these discussions, just as my discussions with my friends, never get anywhere. Mostly, I have concluded, this is because by the time the third or fourth round of drinks is served, somebody is sure to observe, "Yeah, but you sureinhell don't want to raise your kids in town, do you?"

No one ever does, so that is that.

After my encounter by the North Shore tracks, however, I decided to look further. Here, after all, was my own youngster drawing on his experience with television westerns to settle in his mind the identity of an ordinary boy. Ordinary? Too ordinary—at least too ordinary to be recognizable within the horizon of a young suburbanite's daily life. Was my young man perhaps an extreme product of sheltered suburban upbringing?

I began to talk to friends, teachers, social workers, guidance counselors, pediatricians, and others who would know. Almost at once, my fears for my own offspring subsided, for here are some of the fully documented incidents I heard about:

A seventeen-year-old girl from a wealthy family was taken to lunch at a downtown department store and didn't know how to get on an Escalator; she had never seen one.

A sixth grader tried to pay for his 35¢ school lunch with a $50 bill.

A normally happy thirteen-year-old girl, on one of her rare excursions into the confusion of the inner city, broke into tears at the unaccustomed sight of an inebriated passer-by.

A seventh grader boasted in school how his father had made him a vice-president in three corporations to satisfy certain technicalities for the income tax authorities.

A lone Negro child in a nursery school was getting along famously, but the parents of the white children were chronically embarrassed because their youngsters kept insisting that the colored child's mother, who called for her boy just like the other mothers, must be the family maid.

An eighth-grade boy told his teacher: "With your talent, why aren't you out in another job making some money?"

And then there was the vignette, so common in Suburbia, that would make the pioneer advocates of child labor laws blush: the newspaper boy who, in inclement weather, is driven over his appointed rounds by Mummy or Daddy in the new family station wagon.

Clearly, it was time to reflect on the way of life that causes the attitudes behind such incidents to flourish.

As so often, statistics barely hint at what is actually a state of mind. True, there are now more of us living in suburbs than live in large cities or in outlying towns or rural areas. The tail has begun to wag the dog. The hordes of suburban children are growing and growing. By 1950, eleven million Americans under the age of twenty lived in Suburbia. Today, there are more than nineteen million—28 per cent of all U.S. children.

More significant is the driving force that makes suburbs proliferate. That force is, simply, escape. Escape from dirt and crowding and switchblade knives and minorities and, well, unpleasantness. Past generations escaped some of it by moving westward, new dangers notwithstanding. Today's enterprising families are dodging problems by fleeing to Suburbia.

Proverbially, many refugees are leaving the city "for the children's sake." This is unquestionably true, but for purposes of later discussion it is well to keep in mind that researchers have now officially isolated a variation on the theme. It is not a commonly accepted one, but a Washington psychiatrist of my acquaintance brought it into the open at a joint conference of the National Institutes of Health and the Brookings Institution on, so help me, "Problems of Migration Among the American Middle Classes." This daring doctor said: "Either you move to the suburbs because you like kids and want things for them, or because the kids are a problem and this will get them off your hands."

I don't know any mothers who usher their kids out of the house in the morning and tell them, "Go out and let the neighbors bring you up." But I have met quite a few ladies who hope that effortless exposure of their children to the wholesome suburban environment and the "nice" parents and kids in the neighborhood will relieve them of some of their own responsibilities.

I am frequently told that suburbs have been with

us for a long time without inspiring much alarm-viewing. True. But most suburbs of pre-World War II vintage are as distantly related to today's subdivisions as the Wright Brothers' first model is to a jet airliner.

Until quite recently, suburbs tended to be little more than privileged but perfectly accessible satellites or enclaves. They depended on central cities. Any child could—and frequently had to—leave them, usually just by getting on a streetcar or a bus jammed with citizens who did not always look and act like the neighbors. But this was before the big population boom, G.I. loans, and the happy spread of affluence prompted builders to lay out bigger and bigger suburbs, equip them with enough services to make them more and more self-sufficient, and move them farther and farther out into the no man's land of yesterday's pastures.

The effect of this new isolation on the orientation of children is little short of staggering. Early in my investigations I discussed this suburban characteristic with the guidance director of a Highland Park grade school. For some years, she had been administering an "interest inventory" to her charges. On the basis of long-term results she estimated that no more than 30 per cent of the children had *ever* visited Chicago's Loop area and only 10 per cent had ever ridden on streetcars, buses, or elevated trains.

"Many, many more have been on planes to Florida and Arizona," she said.

Here is a fairly typical by-product of the suburban way of life. It is not exclusive to the new Suburbia. No doubt some children have been similarly sheltered in the past. And no doubt there are kids in non-suburban environments today growing up in relative isolation from the world around them. But like most of the problems we will examine shortly, removal from reality affects far more youngsters than ever before and it is greatly *intensified* by today's suburban setting.

Suburban youngsters who are now barely in their teens are a very distinctly new breed. They are the first generation to be reared by the subdivision experience. The term "subdivision," moreover, requires amplification. It has become declassé, of course. Many suburbanites deny that they live in a subdivision. But we are not concerned with the nomenclature of real estate men. The point is that most of Suburbia lives in a subdivision frame of mind, and for an excellent reason: Suburbia has quite literally subdivided the country.

While most of us were not looking, a little-noted process began to fission away out in the now-so-distant suburban acres. It was nothing less momentous than a reshuffling of much of the population of the United States. If we were once a melting pot, we are no longer. The ingredients in the pot are separating and congealing.

Historically, suburbs have ever been select oases attracting migrants who were in search of their own. As long as these class-conscious segments were small and within easy reach, the impact on their children was tempered. Now that the same sifting process engulfs millions, more and more kids come to know only their neatly manicured, fumeless, comfortably monotonous bedroom communities where there are almost no old people, no poor, no childless, no Negroes, either no Jewish families or many, no sidewalks, no places to explore except by mother-chauffeured car, no houses or incomes too different from those of their parents.

"We seem to be stepping into a new ghetto," I was told by Dr. Donald H. Bouma, a young Grand Rapids, Michigan, sociologist, who was one of many knowledgeable researchers I consulted. "The suburban group loves it that way. It puts a protective armor around them."

Exactly how standardized are the new communities that are everywhere sprouting, more or less full blown, out of the ground after shade trees and other impediments are carefully cleared away?

The YMCA wanted to find out. Its leaders recognized that more and more of Suburbia's privileged offspring are stranded in the sticks, deprived of many recreational facilities which, once upon a less prosperous time, beckoned right next door in the now out-of-style city neighborhood.

I'm delighted that the "Y" people have discovered that somebody out there loves them. I know my own boys do. For them, it is the acme of bliss to be transported, of a blue and mellow Sunday, to an unsanitary area downtown and "the 'Y' with the big gym." As soon as they arrive at this sweaty Mecca, they throw themselves into their gym clothes and revel in the atmosphere like bantamweights bursting to get back into the ring after a long, involuntary retirement between bouts. They swim and trot around "the real track." They gape at the real live men puffing and grunting under staggering weights and test their own muscles on various greasy gadgets. All these feats are performed at top speed because the boys know that soon it's time to journey home and the next such excursion is a long time off, as a kid's calendar creeps. It's next to impossible to shoo them, bone-weary but beaming, out of the distinctly unfashionable building.

Well, the "Y" decided to look over its potential clients in Streamwood, Illinois, on Highway 19, eleven miles east of the industrial city of Elgin. Three years prior to the 1959 survey, Streamwood had been a gleam in a subdivider's shrewd eye. By the time a team of "Y" surveyors interviewed 234 families—about one-quarter of the population—1020 houses had gone up. Another 1000 homes a year were scheduled to be built and before long Streamwood would reach its predestined population of 25,000.

The homes ranged in price from $13,500 to $18,000. "There are eight basic styles with 30 variations and modifications possible," the "Y" report stated. The basic styles in families offered less variety. Only three households were without children and of the 737 children surveyed only nineteen were teen-agers. No children were seriously overworked. In only six families did they mow the lawn and in just eleven households they helped with the dishes.

About three-fourths of the families had spent most of their lives in nearby Chicago or surrounding towns. Now, the fathers drove to work a median distance of seventy miles, round trip. Only twenty-seven classified themselves in professional categories more elevated than "foreman-supervisor." College graduates numbered 16.2 per cent among the fathers and 11.3 per cent among mothers; yet 75.1 per cent of the parents expected all their children to graduate from college. Only one parent specified that he wanted his youngster to be anything but a white-collar success. This singular realist wanted his boy to "be a good mechanic." On our travels through Suburbia we shall not meet his like again.

Among the families disclosing religious preferences, 129 were Protestants, 84 Catholics, none Jewish. One classified himself as "atheist," another act of unsuburban courage.

Although almost all (88 per cent) of the Streamwood families were living in the first homes they had ever owned, only fourteen bothered to profess that they moved there because they "liked the community." When they were asked what "most influenced your locating in Streamwood?", the vast majority responded with "price of homes" or "low down-payments" or "best quality of homes for the price" or "liked looks of home." Other popular reasons were: "Better environment for children to grow up" and "more room needed for family."

Now that they had presumably achieved one of the central goals of their lives, how firm were their new roots? About one-third confessed that if they had the chance to make the choice again, they would move some place else. About the same number said "No" when they were asked, "Do you plan to live here until your children complete high school?"

Everyone who has ever lived in a Streamwood—or its more advanced equivalent with $40,000 houses—knows that in these green and gracious places everybody's business is everybody else's business and attitudes are as contagious as the latest type of stomach virus. It is less often realized that the constantly increasing physical isolation of the suburb from the city has created a phenomenon which our society has never known on a significant scale: the one-class community.

There is no need to take my word for this. When I began my research, the Golden Anniversary White House Conference on Children and Youth was about to be held. I attended, listened among the delegates and found them considerably exercised about the peculiarities of "organization children." A workshop of educators and planners actually passed a resolution deploring the "cultural deprivation" of suburban youth.

One of the background papers prepared for the Conference was called "The Effects of Suburban Living." Its author was Dr. Dan W. Dodson and it encapsules more solid fact and good sense than I have read on this subject before or since.

Here are a few of its highlights:

"In the past decades the urban place dominated the suburbs. Today the suburbs dominate the city. . . . 'Suburbanism' has become the style pattern for the total society. That which is smart, chic, worthy of emulation, is suburban. The symbols are the station wagon, the cook-out and a lawn mower which one can ride. . . . Resident families have comparable incomes and comparable social status. There are few relatives, such as uncles, aunts and grandparents to provide a link with other generations and older cultures. . . . *The one-class community does not provide the child with a realistic picture of the world around him. . . .*"

I talked for quite a while with Dr. Dodson, a huge, relaxed former Texan who turned out to be a father of two teen-agers, professor of education at New York University, director of its Center for Human Relations and Community Studies, and a suburbanite who was about to move back into an apartment.

"The kids are getting most problems only out of books," he said wistfully. "They've learned to handle life with a poker."

Dr. Dodson confessed that in most groups where he had had occasion to bring these matters up, people were inclined to look at him a trifle oddly. I soon discovered, however, that he and I and the White House Conference delegates were not alone in our ruminations. In fact, just about every qualified authority who has ever taken a long look at suburban children emerged with similar apprehension.

The most detailed study was conducted by a team of three Canadian social scientists who concluded in their 505-page analysis of a Toronto suburb, "Crestwood Heights: A Study of the Culture of Suburban Life": "The Crestwood child has been constantly urged by his parents and teachers to become mature and responsible, but the culture has not provided many opportunities to become either in reality."

Dr. Leonard Duhl, a psychiatrist at the National Institute of Mental Health, told me that in his opinion most suburban kids are bound to wind up with a caricaturelike picture of life. Perhaps the best picture of suburban disillusionment comes from a Harvard anthropologist, Dr. Dorothy Lee, who described her return to the city at a seminar at Goucher College in Baltimore:

"I fled, not from the country, but from the filtered experience which I had been providing for my children. We went to where the children could be tempted to join street corner society, where they could see brute

poverty, and vice and exultation, and the bewilder-
ment of the rejected immigrant; where they could be
exposed to bad English and despicable music. I took
them where they could meet taste that had not been
labeled good or bad, so that they could make their
own decisions about it; where their associates had not

been implicitly pre-selected and pre-labeled as desirable . . .

"This is not to say that a girl in the city would end up by having a different assortment of friends than she would have had in the suburb. The point I want to make is that in the city she would have arrived possibly at the same kind of friends after having lived through the experience of choice, through perhaps the anguish of rejection and the doubts revolving around selection, and thus would have grown as a person. . . . She would have created her own experience and she would have been an agent in her own existence."

The suburban experience, too, involves choices, but these are necessarily much more limited and the resulting field of vision is much narrower. Right close to home, in Highland Park, I found confirmation. Mrs. Martha Winch, director of the local Family Service, said she found many of her adolescent callers "provincial" and afflicted with "tunnel vision." Dr. Gustave Weinfeld, Highland Park's only child psychiatrist, agreed and pointed to the stimulus provided by Suburbia's false values.

"The big difference about suburbs is the struggle for status," he said. "The child sees his parents struggling to belong to the best country club. When he gets to high school, he struggles for the same status. If he isn't accepted by the so-called 'wheels,' it can have a devastating effect."

Some thoughtful parents have begun to see psychological pot holes between the crabgrass. "There is a monotone of emotions," one father said. "The kids almost never see a funeral. Death has become impersonal. Maybe that'll make it difficult for them to show and feel emotion later on."

A mother said: "There's no place here to make a mess. Everybody keeps the yard just so. There's no place where kids can go dig a hole, no sidewalks to ride on, no fences to climb."

The feeling of temporariness—of an almost open-end life—never leaves many suburbanites. "We always say we're going *home* to Iowa for Christmas," said a teacher who hasn't lived in Iowa since his teens.

Even some of the older youngsters I interviewed said they miss access to ample parks and good libraries. "If you don't have a car there are fewer places to go than in town," said one teen-ager. But if ever there was a minority opinion, this was it. For it is one of Suburbia's whopping dividends that almost every youngster loves it there. Almost every interview shows it: "I've got a lot more friends here." . . . "I just don't like being crowded and all the noise." . . . "We couldn't go anywhere in the city because the neighborhood was real rough." . . . "It's quiet here and clean and new and fresh." . . .

There are, of course, many capital assets for children in Suburbia, and we will examine them later in our travels. Geographically speaking, our movements will not be ambitious. The suburban sensitivity, as we'll observe, is such that I have decided to play the game by the most conservative rules possible.

We have now glimpsed some of the problems. We have listened to some of the experts. For our more clinical examinations, we will forego an invasion of the Connecticut advertising men's exurbs, where a pig-tailed urchin was once pointed out to me by an awed adult who whispered: "Do you know who *she* is? Her father wrote 'Duz does everything!'" Nor will we peer under the froth of the water-ski cultures of Florida or California. We will, instead, stay for the most part in the hotbed of normality, the easy-going midlands where, it is often said, good hard common sense is imbedded in the very grass roots.

I have picked two guinea pig communities, largely because they seem to have so little in common and because no major aspect of either one can be considered extreme. Neither community is a suburban cliché, such as Streamwood. So it cannot be glossed over that the sentiments prevailing in these two suburbs are not only close to identical but were often voiced in identical language! As we go along, then, I will less frequently specify which bit of intelligence originated in which community. There really is no need for it. In fact, I defy the reader to match a given attitude with its place of birth.

For our upper-bracket specimen, I have decided to stick with Highland Park, a relatively heterogeneous community with a fair-sized, old-time central business district and an untypical religious melting pot composed of an estimated one-third Protestant, one-third Catholic, and one-third Jewish families. About an hour north of Chicago by train and car, it is a long-established commuter town which grew from a population of 14,476 in 1940 to 16,808 in 1959 but then boomed to 25,600 by 1960. The median family income is $13,007. Community services and spirits are of a high order. Most of the fathers are business or professional men. Few mothers work.

But the one-class (or one-attitude) community is

not necessarily an upper-class community. We will discover this in our Comparisonville: Bellefontaine Neighbors, a half hour's car ride north of St. Louis. In 1950, it was open fields. At the time of my last visit the population exceeded an estimated 20,000. There was one Jewish student in the junior high school. The city was run, largely by part-time officials and momentum, from its fifth temporary city hall, a two-bedroom ranch-type home which it rented for $130 a month. However, let no one hint that Bellefontaine Neighbors is not trying to "get with it." At the supermodern new school administration building I was shown a vacant office.

"That's for the psychiatrist," my guide said with pride.

Most Bellefontaine Neighbors homes ranged in price, when new, from $11,000 to $17,000 and some cost up to $30,000. The two shopping centers are lost in four square miles of neatly lined-up, sun-baked houses. Most of them are owned by men who work in breweries and factories or who attained white-collar status not too long ago. Incomes were estimated at just about the national average—between $6000 and $6500. This includes earnings of many mothers (some say as many as 50 per cent) who must work, often just to keep up with the costly tastes conditioned by their neighbors and children.

I'll concede that it seems preposterous to expect Bellefontaine Neighbors and Highland Park parents to bring up their children, in all important respects, along identical lines. Well, the reader will recall the series of anecdotal sample coddlings cited early in this chapter.

All of these originated in Highland Park. Now here are some from Bellefontaine Neighbors:

A four-year-old was taken by his mother to St. Louis, where he spotted a Negro boy and said, "Look how dirty that boy's face is!"

A housewife who lived on Waldorf Street said, "I'm known as 'The Witch of Waldorf.' I make my kids walk a mile to school."

Two boys, aged ten and fourteen, were taken by their father past some downtown slums. One of the boys demanded incredulously, "You mean people *live* in these places?"

A mother took her six-year-old to a parade in the city. Several urchins were following a street vendor and occasionally managed to snatch some popcorn that spilled onto the street. The suburban six-year-old asked, "Why are they picking the popcorn off the street?"

Harvard's Dr. Lee captured the picture sharply in her talk at Goucher College:

"For a suburbanite more so than for a city dweller, experience comes filtered and pre-ordered. The range of experience has been pre-selected and highly narrowed. The goal of efficiency is more than elsewhere realized here. And, in the suburb, no less than in the city, the individual is viewed and dealt with as a representative of a category, rather than as a person in his own right.

"If we are to speak the language of the existentialist, I would say that all this spells alienation to me. The individual is set on a track which leads and moves him away from encounter with the data of experience. He is provided with a life which does not evoke the exertion of the self; a life which does not call forth commitment. Since experience comes to a large degree pre-fabricated, the individual is not incited to engage himself in the process of living, to take on his responsibility of choice, and his role as agent. This I believe to be more true of the suburbs than of the city. If suburban life is 'paradise regained,' it is, to my mind, the wrong kind of paradise."

2. *What Ever Happened to Daddy?*

One of my favorite *New Yorker* cartoons depicts two moppets sitting disconsolately on the immaculate front lawn of an ample suburban residence. One moppet is saying to the other, "I don't know what my father does all day. All I know is it makes him sick at his stomach."

When I first spotted this social commentary I did a double-take and hurried to the notes I had taken during interviews in Highland Park months before. There was something eerily familiar about the cartoon caption. And no wonder. A social worker had told me:

"The child here does not know what the father does. Most of us could see him at his work, maybe in the office. Now father's job is just in the clouds somewhere. All the child knows is that his father is crabby when he comes home."

Of all the concealed costs of suburban living, this is the steepest—and the least discussed: just as the configurations of the new suburbs set off an unscrambling and stratification of the population, so there has occurred, while most of us were preoccupied elsewhere, a fundamental reshuffling within the family. A briefing paper for the 1960 White House Conference on Children and Youth put it bluntly: "In the suburb the parental roles undergo considerable alteration. The mother becomes the authority figure of the family, since the father is away for such extended periods of the day."

Few changes in our modern society exercise greater impact on children than this subtle shift of responsibilities right in the home. A close look at the *dramatis personae* and the mechanics of the resulting upheaval is indicated.

There are few irresponsible fathers in the suburbs. Quite the contrary. The men who shoulder Suburbia's mortgages, psychic and otherwise, tend to be intelligent, hard-working, ambitious, on-the-way-up. Again and again I heard them described as "pushers," and it's an apt label. Quite a few of the "sacrifices" they offer in order to move to the suburbs are rendered to soothe their own cravings for peace and status, yet their feelings for their families are almost invariably strong.

Necessarily, however, these men are victims of the suburban circumstances. Little elaboration of these circumstances is needed here except the reminder that they often stretch from coffee-on-the-run just as the children get up, to martinis-on-the-rocks just as the children go to bed. Out-of-town business trips are routine. Perhaps not since our forebears adjusted their armor and rode off to the Crusades, have so many children seen so little of so many fathers.

The absentee father is missed in different ways at the different age levels of the children.

A Highland Park grade-school guidance director said: "I ask the children, 'What kind of things do you

do with your Dad at home? Does your father ever play with you? Does he take you any place?' The answers are dismal. Most of the fathers get home late. They're involved in community projects. They're presidents of this and that. The kids see Dad reading the newspaper, looking at TV, and going to work."

A high-school guidance counselor said: "The father missing from the home in Suburbia will have far-reaching effects on the suburban male. He doesn't know his father. They don't have small rituals together, maybe even like when they wash their faces. It's the atmosphere. Boys have told me time and time again they have no male figure to identify with."

A high-school vocational counselor reported that when he discusses a choice of college or future career with youngsters he often finds them, in effect, father-less: "I ask them, 'How do you suppose your father would feel about this?' They say, 'I don't know.' I ask them, 'How do you mean?' They say, 'My father is never home. I don't really know my father.'"

In Bellefontaine Neighbors, the story is the same.

A guidance counselor said: "The father is out working, pushing all the time. A lot of the kids may say, 'Father runs the family,' because it's the accepted thing. But it may not be the case. They don't believe father is the boss."

As a seven-year-old of my acquaintance once said with the candor of his age: "Mummy is the boss and Daddy carries the luggage."

Dr. Norman R. Loats, the assistant superintendent of schools, agreed that the mother-father switch poses a critical problem and added thoughtfully: "I shouldn't talk. I'm as guilty as anybody. I'm just gone, gone, gone. I eat dinner in the kitchen snack bar because of my evening schedules. As a kid I had dinner for one and one half hours and nobody was in a hurry to go anywhere. Is this the price we're paying for getting ahead?"

Dr. Loats and other worried observers note, too, that the age when fathers drive themselves hardest to get ahead is also the time when their children are small or adolescent and need fathering most.

The children are acutely aware of what they're missing. When a school in Westchester County, New York, assigned 103 pupils aged eight to twelve to write unsigned compositions on "Looking at My Parents," the cry for Daddy kept recurring.

"My father works and has no time to go places with me," wrote one child.

"I would like to paint the house when my father does," wrote another.

"My Daddy asks me again and again if I need eny (sic) help with my work. I always say no," another related. "And when I need help he won't do it with me."

"I would like to go fishing and crabbing more often

in the summer," went another plea. "They always say, 'I haven't any time.'"

The experts are most concerned about the effect of absentee fathers on the future development of boys. As the Canadian Crestwood Heights study points out, suburban children quickly learn that their parents' time for them is strictly rationed. It adds: "The boy is likewise deprived of a male model with which to identify himself . . . and thus learn at firsthand the masculine role in the culture."

A social worker put the matter to me more succinctly: "A boy like that may grow up to bake a fine cake, but he won't be much of a boy."

The lack of male "models" is intensified by the prevalence of lady teachers in the schools. Some, like the Evanston, Illinois, public school system, are becoming aware of the need for more masculinity in the classrooms of commuter children. Evanston, which has launched a campaign to attract more male teachers, reported that only eight per cent of the present staff are men. It would like to see the figure raised to 50 per cent, but progress is of necessity slow. In most areas the problem is not fully recognized and remains neglected.

Pediatricians and psychiatrists are tut-tutting about a whole range of typically suburban phenomena which add up to a blurring of sexual differences among parents that cannot help but confuse children. What about all the housewives who wear pants, perform rugged chores around the house, and call themselves Billy or Sydney? What notions about femininity will a little girl glean from a mother who acts much of the time in a bi-sexual capacity?

Daddy's schedule being what it is, Mummy takes over many of the routine male duties of a less advanced society. She is also forced to assume much of the all-important function of administering discipline. Fathers become bogy men. Their glowering image is trotted out by

the mothers only in cases of dire emergency ("If you don't . . . I'll tell Daddy!"). When youthful scholastic failings are at issue, the fatherly reactions can become particularly severe, as we'll have occasion to discuss in detail later on in connection with what I have come to call The Great Expectations Syndrome.

Generally, one difficulty is that most phantom fathers don't become involved in problems of discipline until after the trouble has ripened into something reasonably serious. Then they are summoned to appear before teachers or principals or psychiatrists, usually before the 8:05 train or evenings or Saturdays. Not having known much about the trouble as it grew, the men tend to over-react and over-punish. This heaps a new burden on the mothers, who must supervise the serving of whatever sentence of punishment is imposed.

At times, the parental helplessness in such situations takes on startling proportions and leads to rather extreme solutions. In one Highland Park home, for example, the mother found it impossible to control her children's television viewing habits. So each morning when the father drove to work, he put the family TV set in the trunk of his car and returned it at night.

The experts agree that the time spent by fathers in the act of fathering is not nearly as significant as the quality of the attention which is imparted to the youngsters. Dr. Weinfeld, the Highland Park psychiatrist, said: "If the father is home for an hour and chucks the kids under the chin, it's better than his being home for five hours and throwing a ball back and forth out of a sense of duty."

Unhappily, time regulates quality in Suburbia. The omni-present "schedule" makes fathering largely a

week-end assignment. And what happens week ends? "It's frenzied," said New York University's Dr. Dodson. "The idea is 'You better make the most of it while you're together.' You have to pursue togetherness too self-consciously." A pediatrician said: "Week ends don't make up the difference. It isn't casual, it isn't relaxed. A lot of fathers are obsessive golfers and they're involved in obsessive entertaining and reciprocating." In one household I know, the kids expressed their frustrations by composing a song. It's called "I Miss You Most When You Are Here."

At a Highland Park junior-high-school band concert

one Sunday afternoon, the band numbered eighty-five and the audience ninety-two. In one public park a pond was stocked with fish for the convenience of the resident fathers. "It's a quick fishing trip, so they can get rid of their obligations to the kids," said a disgusted policeman.

Sometimes the fathers unwittingly transfer their own drives and anxieties to the children. In Bellefontaine Neighbors, the Khoury League, an aggregation of junior baseball teams, had morale problems for a while because the daddies were so keen to manage only winning teams that many kids warmed the bench all season.

Many a father will be both surprised and delighted to learn that the nation's suburban experience has indubitably proved him—or somebody like him—to be essential to his children. So essential, in point of fact, that an unceasing talent hunt in search of tolerably satisfactory stand-ins is in progress throughout Suburbia.

"Teachers have become mother substitutes and father substitutes," a Highland Park guidance counselor said in a typical lament. "Mothers come in to see us for reassurances they should be getting from their husbands. They want to know how to handle the child and how to get him to study? Why doesn't he get home after school? They want reassurance that their rules are good rules and they want to know how to enforce them."

Pediatricians also find themselves drafted for father duty. "I repeatedly go into households where there is a medical crisis," one doctor reported. "The mother is insecure and alone. A child can't get dependent support from a mother who doesn't get it from a husband. The pediatrician becomes a guardian-father. He gives the mother dependent support so she can give the kid dependent support."

Police officers and clergymen are among others who increasingly resent being burdened with parental responsibilities, and so are maids. A principal said: "One colored maid told me the other day, and I think she was speaking for all the maids in Highland Park, 'These people here go off to New York and the Bahamas and we're supposed to take care of their kids. We can't do it!'"

In Bellefontaine Neighbors, where there are almost no maids, the parental void is more likely to be filled by an older child.

"I do all the normal things that every husband does," I was good-naturedly informed by a seventeen-year-old boy whose father's furniture business forces him to be out of town a good deal.

If fathers are compelled to neglect the "normal"—or basic—family duties, it is natural that certain fringe benefits, once furnished by the less successful daddies of another time and place, also elude many children. I refer particularly to conversation. Specifically, the answering of questions cascading out of curiosity-ridden little minds.

The mothers of my acquaintance, by and large, perform ceaselessly and intelligently at this important and frequently taxing task. To an extent which many of us have not yet grasped, the ladies are implicitly supplemented—tirelessly and often shockingly—by the settings, action, and dialogue of "situation comedies" and other

TV programs that flood daily through the eyes and ears of Junior America.

To a child, however, especially a boy, no substitute has yet been devised for some intimate "yakking" with Daddy. My own children, for instance, are endlessly fascinated with explanations of preposterous photographs of me as a child, my less than heroic service as a sergeant in the United States Army, my pitiful athletic achievements, and other (to me) meaningless details of my youth.

Given a chance, they also express embarrassingly detailed interest in my relations with my bosses and such questions as the need for business lunches ("You call that work?") and what items are allowable on expense accounts and why. They want to know what sort of work my secretary helps me with and they like nothing more than to come to my office, sit at my desk and pound my typewriter.

They could not readily get this sort of briefing from anyone else, and I know now, hopefully not too late, how important it is that they do get it. For at stake is even more than an opportunity to make them aware that the life I lead may soon be their own. It is also a matter of helping them *belong*—to an age group, a family, a sex, a continuum of life which starts at an identifiable place and progresses through amazingly logical stages to a preordained end.

Despite its widely advertised "roots" it isn't easy to *belong* in Suburbia, except to masses of equals. For in their flight away from unpleasantness most suburbanites have left in-laws, grandparents, and other aging relatives in a distant part of town or, often, in some thoroughly unsuburban place hundreds or thousands of miles distant.

The sociologist has his jargon to describe this pulling apart of the generations. "There is little opportunity for the validation of self in Suburbia," said one. "Children wonder, 'Where do I come from?' 'Where am I going?' 'What was Daddy like as a boy?' 'What's it like to be old?'"

And so, by the process of elimination, we have arrived at the inescapable: that Suburbia, to most of its children, spells MOTHER.

Let's have a look at the lady.

3. Isn't It Nice
That He Doesn't Have to?

The lady in mink stepped out of the convertible at the supremely expensive Miami resort hotel, so the story goes, and gave the doorman firm instructions. She wanted all of her suitcases removed from the car with care. She wanted special attention paid to her hat boxes. And she wanted her son carried upstairs to his room.

The doorman looked at the boy, estimated that he was about thirteen years old and said:

"But, Madam, can't the child walk?"

The lady in mink replied:

"Of course, but isn't it nice that he doesn't have to?"

I'm certain that this apocryphal lady was vacationing from the rigors of Suburbia. I'm sure of it because over-protective mothers rule the roost in the suburbs, and it is easy—and somewhat unfair—to lampoon them. For their attitudes, like those of their husbands, are to a considerable degree the inevitable consequence of suburban circumstances.

Let's first remember the environment in which the mothers operate. Not only is it bland. It was pains-

takingly designed in the dreams of its residents to *be*
bland. The suburban architects, planners, and builders
only filled in the details. Like any responsive enter-
prisers, they knew what the customers wanted. They
knew that nearly all of Suburbia's settlers are escapees
from the city. These customers were fleeing from the

city's tumult and strife. They wanted life to be more "quiet," "clean," "fresh," and "new." Even their kids use these words when they are asked to describe Suburbia in contrast with the city.

The newness of it all enabled the suburbanites to create an environment in their own image. The Pilgrims, of course, were equally privileged to "roll their own." But their tastes and their technology were of a somewhat different order.

I trust it is no longer necessary to re-emphasize that we are not merely inspecting Highland Park and Bellefontaine Neighbors. We are exploring the suburban soul. Highland Park and Bellefontaine Neighbors are our laboratories. But just to be positive that we are not bogging down in detours away from Suburbia's main stream, it is instructive to glance northward from time to time to check what the Canadian explorers found in "Crestwood Heights."

So here is what they have to say about the setting of *their* laboratory and its effects on young Toronto suburbanites:

"The thermostat of the Crestwood house maintains an even temperature within the house, and the child is protected from the elements when he is outside by raincoat, snowsuit, station wagon coat, and the like—which are provided without effort on his part. . . . He must, it is true, learn the hazards of automobile traffic, but these are gadget-derived threats, and hence, to him, ultimately controllable. To this child, nature is seldom either beneficent or threatening. His milk comes out of a bottle; his fruit out of a basket. . . ."

This, then, is Mummy's battlefield.

Let us next recall that she has been deprived of

much husbandly support. At the same time, as we shall see later, she has a strong inner need to protect her brood from the harsh realities which she herself confronted in her own less comfortable childhood. We'll also have opportunity to dissect with some care how she and her children—whom she adores and thinks and constantly frets about—come under formidable pressures from the community. The upshot is that Mummy does what comes naturally. She mothers. She over-mothers.

Physical pampering is the initial step in the sheltering process. Deploring the flabbiness of youthful muscles has become a national pastime, and surely this manifestation of our New Frontier affluence is not confined to Suburbia. But, like so much else that is being expertly deplored in our national life, soft young body tissue flowers in the suburbs in its lushest form.

"We have a lot of kids who can't chin themselves twice," said a junior-high-school principal. When word got out that he had confided this to me, a group of boys marched into the gymnasium to "show 'em." They tried to chin themselves twice—and couldn't.

At Highland Park High School it was once required that the older boys run the mile in under six minutes. The rule was quietly dropped. It was controversial—a very nasty word in Suburbia. "We got so many repercussions that we gave it up," a counselor said. "We didn't want to take the beating from the parents."

Vitamins, sunshine, and plenty of steak notwithstanding, many boys' physiques tend to be less hardy than those which their underprivileged fathers, in their less scientific youth, developed on starches and similar now un-American ingredients. "The boys' legs look like the girls' legs," a former coach commented. One of the popular *bon mots* of the athletic director at Highland Park High is, "You can't build muscles by slamming Cadillac doors."

Exaggerated mothering leads to exaggerated apprehensions of physical injuries. "I used to coach football," a teacher said. "The smallest kind of injury, like a sprained thumb, was a crisis. Once we had a *broken* thumb. The kid showed up with a cast to the elbow and said, 'My mother insisted.'"

Oh, and how Mummy despises germs! "When I call up and say a child has even a slight temperature, the mother is there right now," said a Bellefontaine Neighbors principal.

While no responsible mother of any generation has ever knowingly wanted a child in school with a fever, the anti-germ cult goes pretty far nowadays. Teachers in Highland Park and Bellefontaine Neighbors agree that the mother-chauffeurs flock to the schools the minute "two clouds get together" when classes are about to let out. "All you need is a sprinkle and there's a mob out there," one said.

Dr. Weinfeld, the psychiatrist, who began his medical career as a pediatrician, observed thoughtfully, "The odd part is that these people know better. They know the kids get colds from one another, not from getting wet."

Some Boards of Education have tried to discourage mothers from descending on the schools in only slightly inclement weather because the practice leads to sizable traffic jams. This is a useless effort to regain reality because it conflicts with another suburban reality. The fact is, as everybody knows, that

all walking is considered *gauche* by just about everyone in Suburbia. In at least one New York suburb an attempt was made to organize walking between home and school. The scheme collapsed, and why not? Don't the children see even maids shuttle to suburban bus stops in taxis? Besides, why shouldn't a youngster consider his ever-willing Mummy a motorized messenger?

"These kids really have their mothers by a ring

through the nose," a doctor said. "If a kid forgets his lunch, mother brings it in the car," a social worker said. "The kid wouldn't think of going back for it."

Motherly efforts to protect children from the man-made threats of their environment are a natural extension of the coddling process. The children are taught to fear traffic. The fathers assist with this instruction and, like the mothers, they're inclined to over-do it. I certainly did with my boys. Not that the lesson isn't vital. Speed limits are notoriously disregarded in many suburbs, mostly by parents. It is easy for a child to be lulled into a false sense of security simply because the restricted area in which he is allowed to roam is clear of traffic much of the time. Again it's the parental over-doing that makes the suburban difference.

Remember the joke about the little boy who was observed determinedly marching up and down the block shouldering a stick from which hung a bundle of his most precious belongings? When a passer-by asked him where he was going, the boy said, "I'm running away from home, but I'm not allowed to cross the street." The story by now has attained something close to folklore status. To me, the significant aspect is that it could never have been told about a kid on the lower East Side of New York.

Like all good jokes, this one distorts real life—but not too much. Consider the ten-year-old boy of a suburban Philadelphia couple I know who sustained a flat tire on his bicycle. His mother told him that she would ask his Daddy to pack the bike in the trunk of the car that night and drive it to a nearby gas station for repairs. Informed of this plan, the father thought that such caution was too extreme and that the child should make his own way to the service station. Reluctantly, the mother agreed. But, by tacit agreement between the parents, the father followed the boy discreetly in the car to be sure that all would go well.

When groups of children are involved, the concern over their safety does not diminish. On busy Green Bay Road, near Highland Park's Edgewood Junior High School, there is an intersection which many youngsters must cross to reach school. The crossing is protected by a traffic light. The light is equipped with a button which the children can push, thereby making all cars stop. No one can remember a serious accident at this location. Yet the parents kept insisting that a patrol boy be stationed at the light to push the button at appropriate times.

Edgewood's principal, Arno Wehle, who happens to be the rare kind of realist who has managed to retain his perspective in Suburbia, refused to furnish the additional protection. But the continuing clamor from some mothers gave him pause. "When kids get to be seventh and eighth graders and can't cross Green Bay Road without getting killed, there's something wrong," he said.

Indeed there is.

When it comes to exposing kids to more distant segments of their world, the caution curve climbs further upward. Rarely do they set foot in the city, much less in small towns or rural areas. "What for?" goes the suburban chorus. "We've got everything right here and in the shopping center." When children do go downtown, the expeditions are carefully planned. Specific destinations, such as museums, are designated as targets. Walks or touring through the city become guided tours through exotic *flora* and *fauna*, with Mummy or Daddy noting special curiosities in the confusing bustle. It took me years to realize that my boys at, say eight or ten, inspected the atmosphere of downtown Chicago and New York like rubes fresh out of the hold of an ancient immigrant transport.

Characteristically, the age at which suburban children should be certified to venture into the city without parental escort is a much-debated point. I discussed this with a group of mothers in Bellefontaine Neighbors. The consensus clearly was that such forays should wait as long as possible because the liabilities of contacts with what penitentiary inmates would call "the outside," it was felt, far outweigh the assets. Indeed, the ladies found it hard to think of any advantages accruing from such ventures at all.

"The first time Jim and some of his pals went on a trip away from home (*sic!*) he was fifteen," related Mrs. Lucille Hedrick, whose husband was an assistant purchasing agent. "They all lost their way. But I don't know that it hurts them to wait to that age. They're learning so much from the schools and the TV programs. They learn about the bad."

"I don't think they're missing a lot," said Mrs. Audria Sgarlata, who was married to a machine shop foreman. "We don't want them roaming on the bus. Our old neighborhood was turning colored and transient. You couldn't walk down the street and feel safe. We've eliminated a lot of these problems now."

Mrs. Isabel Williams was in general agreement, although she and her husband, a metallurgist, had no hesitation in letting their fifteen-year-old son roam for weeks through Europe on a well-chaperoned tour of youth hostels.

Paul Stergos, a Bellefontaine Neighbors grade-school principal, was alarmed at the prevailing hesitancy of parents to relax supervision gradually. "It isn't giving the children a chance to think on their own," he said with some heat. "When are these kids going to get on their own damned feet and learn to make a few decisions by themselves?"

It was, as Stergos well knew, a rhetorical query. In Suburbia, children turn into decision-making adults overnight. Just like that. The event occurs on a quite specific and predictable day. It is, as we'll consider subsequently, the day when they or one of their close friends begin to drive a car. The power of this mechanical contrivance is rarely realized by parents until this event is upon them. The social preparation for it is usually correspondingly meager.

A couple I know in suburban Clayton, Missouri, has a fourteen-year-old daughter who was dating a fourteen-year-old boy. It is the family custom for the father or mother to drive the couple to the movies, to pick them up from the movies, to drive them to a drive-in ice cream stand and then home. At the drive-in, the boy and girl get out. Mother or father sit in the car, like the liveried chauffeurs of yesteryear.

Authority to drive on their own removes the children's relationships with others, for the first time in their lives, from the more or less effective regulation of the parents. Unfortunately, most mothers have been working like beavers during the kids' previous life span to protect them—and not simply from nature, germs, traffic, and the evils of the sooty city. Until fairly late in

3

the maturing process, Mummy has also been sheltering the children from each other.

"The mothers settle all the arguments," Paul Stergos said. "They say, 'You come inside and *you* go home!' They won't let the children handle their own problems." Most principals with whom I talked agreed heartily.

"They won't let the children take their own knocks," said one. "There's less fighting that way, but it's peace at any price." A minister's wife said she had noticed the maternal hovering in the playgrounds of the little ones. "There's always an adult bossing the job," she said.

John Cecil, a seventeen-year-old at Riverview Gardens High School in Bellefontaine Neighbors, volunteered: "If a mother sees somebody fighting somebody, she jumps out of the house and then it's 'Don't you touch little Joey!' Well, he's going to have to learn to protect himself. Maybe the mother should watch and just make sure he doesn't get hurt too much."

The teen-agers sense what the parents are trying to accomplish. "I don't think they're spoiling us," said sixteen-year-old Sandy Gattermeir, a twelfth grader at Riverview Gardens. "They're protecting you. They're trying to protect you from the blows they know you're going to get."

A surprising number of her contemporaries recognize this parental yearning. They even admire it. But they suspect that, like much else in their gentle environment, it is just a little out of this world.

4. Shaking the Money Tree

According to a gag reported from the New York suburbs, a father came upon his ten-year-old lighting a
cigarette with a flaming $10 bill. Aghast, he said,
"Junior, how many times have I told you that smoking is bad for you?"

The fact that this story made the rounds is encouraging because it indicates that suburban parents are beginning to search seriously for answers to a chronic dilemma. Over and over again, I heard it stated in the same words, "The kids don't know the value of a dollar."

In my talks with groups of teen-agers the search for an explanation rarely took too long.

"We haven't been taught," said a pretty and poised sixteen-year-old brunette.

How to teach the value of money, however, is a multi-dimensional problem.

Money, alas, belongs in the realm of reality, and of this there is not much within the grasp of the suburban child. He doesn't normally see what Daddy must go through to earn his dollars. Much less can he divine what a truck driver must do to earn enough to buy himself, or his youngsters, a pair of shoes.

The suburban child hears a good deal of talk around the house about periodic shortages of money, but these conversations make little sense to him. If Daddy is out of dollars, how come he can afford a second car which he drives to the station and leaves there all day where it's of no use to anybody? How come he and Mummy can buy plane tickets to go to Florida? If money is so scarce and so almighty, how come his parents can buy most anything by showing the clerks in the stores a small card and signing the sales slip? Why does everybody keep lecturing about the value of saving money when it's obvious that there is always more where the last supply came from? Most puzzling of all, can money truly be short if a kid can frequently squeeze more cash or more presents out of his parents just by whining and wheedling long enough?

The resulting confusion ultimately infects more than attitudes toward dollars and cents. I learned this in the home of friends in suburban Washington, D.C. The teen-age daughter in this household had been getting an allowance of $5 a week. Then, during school vacation, she commendably got a job paying $67 a week. Nevertheless, she expected her allowance to continue and considered it rather unreasonable when her parents decreed otherwise. The parents, in turn, were a little shocked themselves.

"You know," said the mother to the father, "I think she'll still want her allowance after she gets married."

She may. For the mystery of this very bright young lady's confusion about the source and value of money goes back almost to the suburban cradle. It begins with that strange parental notion about spinach (or carrots or peas, etc., etc.). Who can seriously believe parents when they claim that spinach does indeed cost enough money to bother about and that a lot of kids in the world have never even tasted any? Isn't it an accepted truth that everybody has more spinach than he can possibly want and who has ever met a single kid that didn't have spinach coming out of his ears?

A police officer in Bellefontaine Neighbors, surveying a world he never made but is now called upon to keep in order, put his finger on the nub of the matter. He said, "Around here, how can you prove to a kid that it doesn't come easy?" A colleague of his, a juvenile officer in Highland Park said, with only mild exaggeration: "We don't have any cars stolen. All our high-school kids got cars."

There did occur, though, an only-in-Suburbia crime wave not too long ago in Highland Park. Groups of adolescents were driving through the streets at night pelting homes and cars with eggs—presumably the "farm-fresh" variety stacked up in the parental refrigerators.

When I brought up the ultra-sensitive subject of presents for the little ones, a pediatrician blew up. "The gifting is just ridiculous," he snorted. "The toy stores around here are really cashing in. The whole thing is unrealistic. There's nothing left to give! They've got it all—toy cars with motors! They cost around $400! It becomes an environmental standard. The kids expect it. My kid, if he doesn't get something, he doesn't see why."

Another doctor diagnosed the wearying cry of "Why can't I?" He felt that it suggests a low tolerance for frustration which will be difficult for many kids to overcome in later life. The doctor said, "Children tell me, 'I don't know why my Dad doesn't buy me a horse. All the kids I know have one.'" Among this young patient's contemporaries you're not in the swim without a winter sun tan, either. And a girl complained to a social worker that she was embarrassed because her "cashmere count" compared unfavorably with that of her cronies.

Some of the boys play poker in the parental recreation rooms, occasionally until two or three o'clock in the morning. Winnings or losses of $10 to $20 per session are routine.

"I know he's doing it," one mother told a police officer, "but he's always winning."

Easy-come-easy-go becomes the standard.

At a Girl Scouts' father-and-daughter dinner in Highland Park's Braeside School, at least half the box lunches had been packed by the same expensive catering service. And quite a few little customers may draw on their own charge accounts at gasoline stations and, yes, delicatessens.

Behold, then, the junior status seeker. A friend of mine took a group of his kid's buddies to a baseball game to celebrate his son's birthday. Obviously, the children were going to be treated to everything reasonable that they might want. Yet all the children showed up with considerable spending money, one boy displaying a $10 bill and noting, "My mother just wanted me to have a little spending money."

It's in the schools' lost-and-found departments that the children's nonchalant approach toward money, and toward the effort required to obtain it, comes into the open at its most dramatic. Just about anything a child handles shows up as lost, but not much finds its way back to the owners. Incredibly, teacher after teacher told me that many expensive items, including watches by the dozen, are never claimed.

One principal decided to make a stand in the case of a beautiful blue cashmere sweater which was turned in with the name of the owner sewn into the collar. He held it for a week. Nothing happened. He then called in the owner, showed her the sweater but kept the name band hidden under his fingers.

"Is this your sweater?"

"No."

"Are you sure?"

"Uh-huh."

Then he displayed the name, and the girl said in real or feigned surprise: "Oh, is that mine?"

The principal told her: "I call that lack of respect for your own property, and I doubt whether you have more respect for the property of other people."

There was no apparent indication whether the lesson hit home or not. Nor is there any reason why it necessarily should have. As another school administrator said, in explaining similar conditions in his jurisdiction, "It's so easy for them to get replacements."

In view of the substantial gap in parental incomes between Highland Park and Bellefontaine Neighbors it deserves to be specifically recorded that the lost-and-found situation in the lower-bracket Missouri community is identical.

"We have glasses, coats, watches, everything—it's amazing," exclaimed an assistant principal. "One kid lost a textbook the other day. It cost $2. He just said, 'OK, charge me.'"

Where the money comes from to finance this kind of waste on $6500 a year is, I confess, not entirely clear to me, although much undoubtedly comes out of the fathers' overtime earnings and the second incomes brought home by many mothers. It is beyond dispute, however, that a Bellefontaine Neighbors high-school senior is not "in" unless he owns a pair of "threads" —Threadneedle shoes of coarse off-white calf's leather tanned in Scotland and costing, the last time I checked, upward of $25.

The youngsters' organized social life does not flourish on quite the scale customary in Highland Park. But the high-school Valentine's Day "Sweetheart Dance" costs a boy $30 to $35, including the pretty much obligatory tuxedo rental. Eighth-grade graduation parties are held in St. Louis' finest night club. Afterward there are further outings with outlays sometimes amounting to $50 and $75 per couple.

In both of our laboratory suburbs, parents are exceptionally touchy about the implication that they might somehow be responsible for actively teaching children a lack of respect for money (which, incidentally, is a charge that most assuredly cannot be raised against the mothers and fathers).

Just how touchy things are in this respect was vividly illustrated in connection with the sixth grader who, as mentioned in Chapter 1, paid for his 35¢ school lunch with a $50 bill. This incident occurred in Highland Park's Edgewood Junior High School. Principal Arno Wehle told me about it and I mentioned it, without naming the school or even Highland Park, in an article in *The Saturday Evening Post*.

The reaction among parents could not have been much more electric if I had accused the unknown parents of this unnamed lad of having given their son lessons in safe-cracking.

Letters of protest were written to *The Post* and to me. Parents' groups took up the case at formal and informal meetings. The variety of explanations that were offered for the appearance of the $50 bill was remarkable.

According to one version, the boy had brought the money to school to pay for a savings bond and was only showing the bill around. According to another account, the boy had earned the money personally by investing shrewdly in stocks and bonds and had brought his profits to school to create a little flurry of excitement.

Still another story had it that he hadn't really brought along a $50 bill at all; that he had been learning all about dividends in class and had brought in a $50 dividend check as a visual aid.

Personally, I may be pardoned for accepting the principal's account. According to Wehle, the boy dropped a $50 bill on the cafeteria cashier's table to pay for a frugal lunch. The cashier called Wehle. Wehle adheres to the quaint belief that small boys ought not to be carrying large sums of money to school. He called the student's mother. She wanted to know what all the fuss was about. It was, she said, the child's money and he could do with it whatever he pleased.

Why is money such a casual item for children in Suburbia, where even quite a few wealthy parents are financially over-extended and definitely not rolling in spare cash?

There are three causes. We have met them before in these pages and we shall meet them again in other contexts. They are:

First, "the Joneses do it" by being overly nonchalant and pressure prone about their spending habits.

Second, the mothers and fathers are determined that their offspring shall not have as "hard" a childhood as they did themselves.

Third, time to pay loving relaxed attention to the children is scarce and money is a relatively easy, guilt-expiating substitute for the parents to distribute. It is no coincidence that the costliest presents are handed out after Mummy and Daddy have been on a long vacation trip while Junior was shepherded about by the maid.

Excessive allowances and other material over-privileges, as the Rev. Russell W. Bletzer informed a seminar on "Adolescence in Suburbia," are really a way for parents to tell their children, "Take this; we haven't time to love you, so this will do instead." Or as a seventeen-year-old boy told me matter-of-factly: "They want so much for their children, but they won't give of themselves."

Money in the hands of Suburbia's children, moreover, is but a symbol. The feeling toward it is a mere reflection of an attitude toward responsibility in general. So this attitude is what we'll pour into our test tubes next.

5. Why Johnny Can't Work

To furnish guidance to the kitchen help at a Highland Park school, teachers obtained from their students daily advance estimates of the number who planned to eat lunch in the school cafeteria. The system worked tolerably well until the estimates more and more frequently turned out to be low, sometimes by as many as sixty.

The overflow came from youngsters who had brought lunches from home but decided at the last minute that they happened to like the school menu better. This might have been no more than a serious inconvenience to the cooks, but investigation by the principal disclosed something more. Many of the kids who had brought their lunches and then turned up their noses at Mummy's handiwork decided to throw their food away. Custodians found the homemade lunches in wastebaskets or more or less successfully flushed down the toilets.

Eventually the principal decided that an object lesson was indicated. After publishing due warning to children and parents, he ordered the school cafeteria closed for one day as a disciplinary measure. The following day the district school superintendent was flooded with calls from outraged parents. Some mothers even began to circulate petitions calling for the firing of the principal. There are, perhaps, more charitable explanations of these parents' motives, but one mother in the faction which sympathized with the principal told me: "They're too darned lazy to make a lunch."

All this is of a piece with another suburban travail: the difficulty of teaching kids a sense of responsibility early enough so it will be firmly anchored by the time they must possess it to cope with the world on their own hook.

The Canadians who studied Toronto's "Crestwood Heights" had this thought-provoking comment: "A boy whose parents cannot afford to send him to college can enter the Air Force for technical training, and to him may be entrusted a costly bomber; the Crestwood boy whose parents can, and do, send him to college, is considered by many parents (and some automobile insurance companies) as an unreliable driver and a poor risk."

Again, we are dealing with a twist of child development that should not really come as a surprise. The gentle, push-pull-click-click efficiency of Suburbia's physical appurtenances has eliminated a lot of the opportunities once available to parents to teach children almost automatically how important (and satisfying) it is to tackle a useful activity, plan its execution, and to stick with it until the job is done.

Labor-saving devices necessarily coddle all but the very smallest citizens. Why should kids be forced to handle garbage pails when most of the refuse in their homes is crunched up neatly and effortlessly by an invisible little machine attached to the patient pipes under the kitchen sink? One bright kindergartener I was told about could not identify a dishpan pictured in her reading test. She had never seen one. Why should she have? Many children in dishwasher-equipped subdivisions haven't.

As the children grow older, quite a few mothers are reluctant to trouble them with the chores that remain with us, at least for the time being. Instead, the drive is all for the children to be "successful," and it is difficult for parents to recognize how in the world proficiency in bed-making will contribute to their darlings' success. If anything, bed-making sounds to the parent like a waste of time, and time-wasting, either by adults or children, why, that is one of Suburbia's ultimate sins.

A sizable proportion of kids, therefore, possibly even the great majority, do not make their own beds. Many boys won't mow the lawn or wash the car without extra pay. I was told of ten-year-olds who went on strike until their daddies got them power mowers. The boys didn't object only to the extra labor involved in hand-mowing. It was the principle of the thing. After all, "everybody" has a power mower.

I collected most of this information from teachers and other adult sources because it isn't easy to persuade the teen-age set to talk candidly about household chores. Fishing for detailed data on this subject is not unlike inquiring about sex habits. It is a point of acute embarrassment. The youngsters feel that admission of their non-laboring habits would stamp them as "lazy." And lazy, as we will shortly document, the

Subdivision Generation certainly is not. In truth, laziness is another vice not tolerated in Suburbia.

Despite the prevailing reluctance, two groups of boys and girls agreed to cooperate with my sampling. In the junior-high-school group, Barry Greis, fourteen, shopped for his mother almost daily, mowed the lawn, and washed the car every other week for 50¢ extra allowance; Kenneth Siemson, thirteen, reported that he did "nothing definite" but swept the basement on Saturdays; Larry Bacon, fourteen, said, "Every other week it's my turn to wash dishes and once every two weeks we clean out the basement"; Sandra Seward, thirteen, reported that her tasks consisted of "nothing regular except I help set the table"; Ricky Unks, thirteen, said he washed dishes every third day and scrubbed the bathroom once a week.

I gained the impression that none of these job descriptions was understated.

In a group of high-school students, two out of five said they made their own beds and helped regularly with the dishes. One girl reported that she helped her mother, who was employed, clean up "on Saturdays." A sturdy lad described his total duties as follows: "Twice a year I have to put up the screens and take 'em down." One girl who performed a solid variety of scheduled chores assigned by her parents volunteered: "If they wanted more, they'd get more."

Teachers complained that they received "hundreds" of notes from parents asking that their children be excused from school because they are "not feeling well," while the kids are actually taking off a day or two from classes to cram for an upcoming exam.

In at least one Highland Park school it was common

practice for parents to help their children type their term papers. One mother asked me earnestly about her boy: "Should I keep him out of a Florida skin-diving trip because he's seven pages short on his paper?" A lot of questions of this caliber are problems of conscience in Suburbia. Luckily, this one was raised during a lively group discussion and I managed to maintain judicial impartiality by switching the talk into other channels.

Many suburban kids do take on summer work but reports about performances on the job are mixed at best. "Some of these boys are real gems and some are little son-of-a-guns," said Dave Fritz, who hired high-school help for Highland Park beaches and parks. But even the "gems" displayed a "considerable amount of independence." To keep life guards on the job through Labor Day, Fritz found it necessary to offer bonuses of $30 to $50 to overcome an annual epidemic of late-summer fatigue.

In Bellefontaine Neighbors, Paul Stergos, an intense, energetic, and popular young principal, was one of numerous critics who felt that the sheltered suburban upbringing generates unhealthy ideas about jobs. At various times, he had worked after school as a variety store salesman, in a brewery laboratory, and as assistant chief usher for a movie chain. Too many of the youngsters he bossed on these jobs, he discovered, lacked initiative, required too much supervision, and blew up with slight provocation.

"I could pick out the suburban types," he said. "They had the attitude, 'If you want me to do something, you'll have to tell me.'" His findings dovetailed with the report of a playground supervisor who said that she often heard little kids ask, "Mummy, what do we do next?" Naturally, Mummy always had a "constructive" answer.

Richard Gray, a guidance counselor who managed swimming pools in the summer, said of his teen-age labor, "They were nice kids, but the level of responsibility they'd accept was practically nil." Allen Pruett, Bellefontaine Neighbors' benevolent police chief, concurred and told of his son turning down a lawn-mowing job to scout about for employment that was "not so sweaty." He found it in a clothing store, where he could wear a white shirt to work.

It's an important item in Suburbia, that white shirt. Success is the thing, and how many people are successful and also sweat?

The urge for the white shirt, of course, originates with the parents. Almost without exception they—and especially the mothers—cherish all signs of early success, social and otherwise, for their kids. "All our youngsters are over-adulted," a school administrator said. "The teen-agers don't plan their own proms. Mother and Dad organize them at the Country Club. Is that teaching responsibility?"

The push starts early. In some neighborhoods dating starts in the fifth grade. Some PTA-sponsored dancing classes begin in the sixth. So do mixed parties featuring kissing games that occasionally even have parental sanction. For the bigger affairs, much attention is paid, even at junior-high-school level, to the quality of the hired entertainment and the sophistication and newness of the girls' dresses.

Sophistication is "in." The Chapel of Grace Lutheran Church in Bellefontaine Neighbors dropped its annual picnic for the first time in 1960. "The kids don't want to go," said Pastor G. E. Nitz, a friendly giant who is the father of seven children. "They're blasé. In the old days it was the big event of the year. Now they have it every day of the week." Eighth graders who don't go steady, said the Rev. Nitz, are considered squares. "It's the fool parents," he exploded. "My wife wants our kids to have boy friends. I say, 'Wait a while, what's the rush?'"

"If they start kissing in the sixth grade, they'll have to get married before high school," speculated Wayne De Beer, principal of the town's high school.

Some of the over-adulting is the result of today's better diet and medical care. Kids mature physically much faster than they once did. The girls menstruate at an earlier age. The architects are putting up the drinking fountains higher in the new schools because the kids are getting taller. But the real pressure to grow up fast comes from the obvious source. A Highland Park guidance counselor said:

"It comes from the home. They're trying to shove experiences down the kids' throats. By the time some of them hit high school, they're already bored to death socially. I know a lot of girls who don't want to go to dancing class. Their mothers force them. And then they force them into cheer leading and on the honor roll. It's too much of a good thing."

With parents inhibiting the step-by-step development of responsibility at the lower end of the growth ladder, and force-feeding the maturation process toward the upper end, the business of growing up becomes more perplexing. Not that it can't be confusing under the non-existent best of circumstances.

The results materialize in the child guidance clinic, on the psychiatrists' couches, and in the police stations —though not as often as one might think. More likely, the confusion surfaces in some pretty silly new folk customs. Some teen-age boys, for instance, don't like to drink. Still, they take liquor along to school dances. Between numbers, they go to the men's room and rinse their mouths with liquor.

"It's sophisticated," said the police officer who told me about it, "and it lets 'em get away with more."

If all this appears to add up to an unsteady picture of well-meaning think-alikes trying their well-meaning best to rear a new generation in a setting which nobody has yet fully understood, then we're on the right track. For this is precisely what is happening.

It is happening, moreover, against a background of a steadily more complex and less comprehensible world which is spawning "experts" in ever-growing numbers. Many of these authorities discourse in tones so convincing that they are credited with knowing all about children. They know what makes delinquents and what to do about it ("Just take the 10-point quiz in the box at the bottom of this page!"). They know that if baby develops an ingrown toenail, Mummy will almost certainly look for it in the index of the proper volume under "T" for "toenail, ingrown." The difficulty is that the experts often disagree about child-rearing problems above the toe line.

Other sources of guidance are teachers, principals, and other experts in the schools. But with certain ornery exceptions, these good people are apt to bend to the collective will of their employers as constituted in the PTA's.

And so, more and more, the wearying parents are beginning to eliminate the middlemen and are trying to help themselves by helping each other. Wasn't it ever thus in grass-roots America? Yes, it was. Only in the New America beyond the city limits, the grass has tender roots, the parents have a tender sense of security, and when they band together to come to the aid of Junior and Sis, the result is. . . .

6. The Junior Rat Race

A suburban pediatrician I know received a call from a mother who announced, "Doctor, I'm dreadfully worried about Susie." When the doctor tried to arrange an early appointment to check Susie, this proved to be complicated. "It turns out she can't make it Wednesday and can't make it Thursday," the doctor told me. "Would you know it? This 'dreadfully worried' mother can't bring Susie in for ten days!"

The case of ailing little Susie, who obviously was not sufficiently infirm to be cause for acute concern, spotlights two characteristics of her species. She is, for one thing, over-protected. She is, for another, over-organized and over-loaded with wholesome pastimes.

At every stop of my suburban travels, teachers and numerous parents (but few kids) complained that the children were so busy being chauffeured to orthodontists, ballet teachers, French teachers, meetings of scouts, ball teams, religious classes, and so many other rigidly scheduled events that they can hardly pause long enough to catch their ozone-rich little breaths.

"They're over-stimulated," said a minister's wife who used to teach school. "They have very little time just to grow up. They never have a chance to be their just plain selves. I think they have a big need to be left alone." In at least one high school, students were being officially warned against the temptation to sample all available after-school activities. "They don't get *involved* in anything very intensively," one teacher said. He disagreed with the dictum of some experts that Suburbia's young are being subjected to a "narrowing of experience." He thought the suburban experience, if anything, is more multi-dimensional than any setting ever created, but that it was "horizontal." Or, bluntly, too shallow to stimulate the growth of inner resources.

A guidance counselor put it like this, "I wonder how in hell these kids ever have a chance for some quiet time for themselves. I think eventually this is going to make this kind of individual awfully miserable if he's ever off by himself or just with his wife."

We have already seen something of the pressure to organize and over-adult the children's social lives. The momentum behind this push is formidable everywhere. In one junior high school, strapless dresses for the girls and caps and gowns for the graduating class were heatedly debated issues. At another, the mothers drafted the principal as a clearing house for the arrangement of the many huge, formal post-graduation parties because the kids' calendars threatened to be overwhelmed by conflicting dates. At a high school, a "make-up class" in dancing was for some time held at 8:30 A.M.

Compulsive? Certainly. And let's be candid and admit that the kiddies were not propelled into this pace by the potency of their Pablum. The opening gun for the rat race was fired by Mummy and Daddy.

"I see a lot of parents who think it's harmful for children to contemplate their navels," a psychiatrist reported. "They consider it wasteful and deteriorating." Frankly, until not so long ago, I was one such parent. Many of my acquaintances still are. "Where are the kids? What are they *doing?*" So goes a popular subdivision refrain. A friend of mine said sheepishly, "Every time we see Lisa sit and doing nothing, we tell her, 'Lisa, for heaven's sakes, go *do* something!'"

The results of this three-ring circus pace are questionable, at least for certain types of children. "If the child is reasonably resilient, he gets along fine," said the pediatrician who tried so valiantly to get an appointment for himself squeezed into the schedule of little Susie, whose mother was so dreadfully worried about her. "If the kid is having any sort of trouble, the pace is too much for him." A social worker in a guidance clinic confirmed, "These kids are just as booked up as their parents are. It makes your head swim. It's too fast a pace for many of them."

Suburban kids, collectively speaking (and is there a better way?), are a sharp bunch. They know what's happening to some of their friends. My own boys speak of these mildly maladjusted contemporaries as "queers" and "retards." And just the other week end, I watched a friend's seven-year-old and ten-year-old play a finger-word game. The seven-year-old said, "Dicky can't. . . ." And the ten-year-old filled in, "cope!"

Not only is the pace unadjusted for the inborn differences of individuals. The kinds of activities that are scheduled are equally standardized. So is the manner in which the activity is pursued. In his book, *"Where did you go? Out. What did you do? Nothing,"* Robert Paul Smith compared his upbringing in New York City with that of his children in a New York suburb. He wrote:

"My kid went to play soccer the other day. The way you play soccer now is this: you bring home from school a mimeographed schedule for the Saturday morning Soccer League . . . There are always exactly eleven men on each team, the ball is regulation size, the games are played on a regulation-sized field with regulation-sized soccer balls, and there is a regulation-sized adult referee."

In contrast, "When I was a kid, the way we played baseball was this: We . . . grabbed a beat-up fielder's glove, went out on the block and met a friend who had an old first baseman's mitt, a ball, went down the block a little and hollered at the kid who had the bat . . . we went to the vacant lot and played a game resembling major league baseball, only that it was played with a bat and bases. It was fun . . . you see it was *our* game. I think my kid was playing someone else's game."

Smith is not the only observer of kids who is mourning for the past. The schools are full of them. "Nothing is very spontaneous any more," said Wayne Pounds, a high-school guidance counselor. "There isn't a thing a kid can do by himself. The home used to be a proving ground. So many of these things have disappeared. They tell you what to wear, when to go, where to go." One of his associates went further, "They've got no free time and they wouldn't know what to do with it if they had it. Fly kites? They're in a club or a team. The pressure is to be like Johnny. There are more than forty clubs in our high school, and there's a gross lack of self-understanding among the kids. They don't know what motivates them."

It's all a bit like drilling regiments of chocolate soldiers, all of whom would melt in the heat at an identical rate.

School materials encourage the new atmosphere where, as has been said, "the bland are leading the bland." A researcher who analyzed manuals for teachers in courses on family life and home economics found that the emphasis was on "getting along." In one lesson on family relationships, the term "get along" was used seven times.

We are zeroing in now on the lack of diversity which David Riesman, in one of his learned papers, has described as "The Suburban Sadness." To be sure, it is a sadness that does not cry out. This, too, would be un-suburban. It is, I think, a negative sadness, more an emotional emptiness. Among the children you encounter it in the form of stunted creativity.

It starts with the very bricks of the ranch house where Junior grows up. The Canadian surveyors of "Crestwood Heights" found these homes almost uniformly "reminiscent of a series of department store windows, charmingly arranged, harmoniously matched in color." The children's rooms were "meticulously fitted to what decorators and the furniture trade consider the taste of a child." The dragging in of horrible junk expressive of a child's personality is discouraged in these well-administered homes. So is the nailing of filthy souvenirs to the walls. After all, most of that one-fifth of a nation that changes homes each year lives in the suburbs, and the resale value of the house must be carefully protected against acts of children who might unwittingly depreciate the family fortune.

"The home becomes a bedroom or a hotel where they come to sleep," said Dr. Leonard Duhl, a Washington suburbanite and a psychiatrist for the National Institute of Mental Health.

"Let's let them dream and create," said a school administrator. "Maybe we ought to organize some daydreaming."

If this were ever done, it surely would be carefully

prearranged for given periods on given days. I doubt whether the kids could handle it otherwise, for never in the history of civilization have there been sub-adults who were so acutely conscious of time. Some of this affinity for the split second was born along with television. What youngster doesn't have his never-missed favorite programs and doesn't know precisely when to throw down the baseball bat and run for home in time to plop himself in front of the screen just after the opening commercial?

Mostly, however, this new dimension of the growing-up process grew either out of the kids' natural tendency to imitate parents or the equally natural parental inclination to guide the children into Mummy's and Daddy's mold. ("Fridays at 9:15 they go bowling," one boy told me, and then he reeled off the rest of the week's hard-breathing schedule of events.)

Parents, in turn, said they wanted their kids to make maximum use of valuable time during the most impressionable years. Most mothers and fathers conceded that they were themselves heavily "goal-oriented," as the experts say, but what was wrong with that? Would they be in Suburbia with a nice house and two cars if they had vegetated in a downtown slum? Parents also reported that they had been scared by experts who advised them to keep their youngsters on the run so that there would be no time for unmarshaled thinking —and juvenile delinquency.

Repeatedly the suspicion was voiced that many parents are excessively preoccupied with their own schedules and therefore warmly welcome an environment outfitted with institutions that are willing to take on part of the chore of raising the kids. Several parents told me, only half in jest, that they were so pre-occupied with rushing to meetings about the welfare of suburban children *en masse* that they had little time for their own.

The drive to deal with youngsters in herds gets its steam, of course, from group pressures. These exist in all communities. But in Suburbia's follow-thy-neigh-bor atmosphere, the pressure is turned on with un-precedented force. One principal said, "You either join up or you're a bum." Another said, "No matter how strongly Mrs. Jones feels her little girl shouldn't go to dancing class, if three neighboring mothers send their little girls, hers becomes ostracized and this is more than a little girl can bear. She'll be frozen out of the group. There are very few mothers who will stand up to that."

The Orwellian aspect of the parental reaction to pressures is the acceptance of the inevitability of it all. The same phrases recur in conversations: "The kids are always on the go." Or, "All I hear is, 'Sandy can, why can't I?' Eventually I give in." And, most frighteningly, "The pace is set."

How can this hothouse atmosphere where "the kids are always on the go" provide a stimulus to sit, to think, to be original, to learn to be as "creative" as the intellectual upper crust of tomorrow will have to be in order to compete and to survive? My informants have every right to wonder, especially since we should not forget that much life experience is acquired, in Suburbia, through pleasantly colored mirrors.

"The individual must create from the source," Dr. Dorothy Lee wrote in "Suburbia: Paradise Re-gained?" "He must see the peas roll for himself, to use Erich Fromm's illustration—not depend on someone else's experience. It is imperative that he create his own experience, perceiving his own pattern out of the chaos. . . . All this is lacking in the suburbs; or, rather, what is offered is just the opposite. . . . Experience is offered organized, pre-labeled, pre-selected, pre-fabricated. . . .

"A teacher in one of the leading colleges told of how she asked a class in literature to read a book about which they had never heard, and report on it. More than half the class came to her and asked her whether it was a 'good book'; because, without knowing this, they did not know how to read it, how to relate to it, what to think of it."

The urge to conform—there, we've said it at last—is infused in the children by the parents via one particularly potent ego-tickler: the ambition to be *popular*. My, how popular it is to be popular in the suburbs! A potential Einstein might never make it to the college entrance examinations under the prevailing scheme of things, but a future Vice-President in Charge of Sales would flourish.

"There is a great premium attached to gregariousness, to being extroverted," said a guidance clinic worker. "When a child happens to be introverted, parents think it's symptomatic of some gross pathology. They're impatient with children who want to be home after school."

The children are expected to clique together, pit themselves against each other in competition, and hold themselves available for group inspections by the mother group. From early childhood on, the little ones have sensed that they, not the adults of their society, are the center of things. Rare is the neighborhood where the mothers are not incessantly congregating to compare notes on the relative attributes and achievements of each other's offspring.

"Everyone wants their children to be popular," they said.

"Nobody wants their children to be wallflowers," they said.

The parents' concern transfers itself to the kids. In the Brooklyn Avenue School of Valley Stream, Long Island, this preoccupation was articulated when a teacher asked her third graders to write, anonymously, their thoughts on three subjects she considered of utmost importance to her charges. These were, "Parents," "Schools and Teachers," and "Why People Should Like Me."

The comments on parents ("They're pretty nutty if you ask me") and schools ("I hate school and I hate teachers") struck me as ageless and routine. The reflections on popularity should not, I think, have been solicited from children who are too self-centered to begin with. But the kids' observations on this subject were unquestionably not routine. Each answer indicated that it had been more thoroughly considered than the comments on the other questions, and that the question itself mattered deeply to each child. Some sample answers ran like this:

"I really don't know why people should like me."

"My friends like me because I am not a big shot."

"I know that nobody likes me and that is all I have to say."

"I am nice and sweet. That is why people like me."

"I guess people like me because I am very nice."

"I try my best but still some people do not like me."

To these children, it seems to me, life is a popularity

contest where the "square," the "odd," the "retard," the non-team player, and, heaven help us, the "unpopular" person will find the going discouraging rather early in the game.

It is, needless to re-emphasize, not a game dreamed up by children or played primarily for their benefit.

"It's a kind of use that's made of the child," said a psychiatrist friend of mine.

Popularity—the earliest symbol of "success"—is in actuality far more yearned for by the parent than by the child, who frequently doesn't even fully understand the term until the age of eleven or twelve. It fills one of the deep needs of the hard-driving but insecure suburban adult. There are more such needs, and they, too, explain why so much that is exaggerated and even outlandish in Suburbia is also inevitable.

7. *Why They Can't Say No*

The biggest word in Suburbia is "They."

It popped up in nearly every conversation and flashed in large mental neon signs in the minds of even the most thoughtful parents—those who readily volunteered that the Junior Rat Race is too frenetic, that there ought to be no "pace" set for their own children by anyone but their own family, and that the pressures to conform are unhealthy.

Among the less thoughtful, too, the suspicion is growing that there is something amiss in what is commonly (and significantly) referred to as "the setup." For instance, I'd bet that a mother couldn't be found anywhere in Suburbia, USA, who would seriously argue—if questioned privately—that semi-formal dances for sixth graders are desirable. Yet invariably, sinister unnamed forces identified only as "they" somehow make it impossible to slow down the suburban merry-go-round, or even the music that accompanies the whirl.

"*They* can't wait for their daughters to have formals," said the mother of an eleven-year-old girl who was about to get her first formal.

A group of four mothers with whom I talked for a long time uniformly deplored the trends to over-adult, over-socialize, over-organize, and over-spend. "I looked at the graduation pictures of these kids," said one of the ladies whose son recently left junior high school. "What have they got to look forward to? These gowns are more beautiful than what they'll have when they get married. If I could, I'd stop it in a minute."

I asked her why she couldn't put her foot down and simply proclaim to all interested parties that her children and their friends are getting too much too soon?

"Nobody has the courage to say so," said this mother. "*They'd* kill me." The other three ladies in the group grinned and nodded agreement. An air of embarrassment had crept into the room. Embarrassment and genuine helplessness.

That same evening, with the help of a PTA president, I convened a larger group of mothers and fathers in Bellefontaine Neighbors to explore further the identity of the mysterious mammoth "They." The antiseptically beautiful new high school sparkled in the evening silence. The modernistic structure was darkened except for the bright lights in our conference room. The assembled parents were perhaps the most sensitive group I encountered during my travels. At first, just as their counterparts elsewhere, they were cautious. Few suburbanites like to hear even the faintest suggestion that possibly, just possibly, not everything is right with their world or—and this is the rawest heresy of all—with the world of their children. But when I brought up what is without doubt one of the heaviest burdens of suburban parenthood, the

75

difficulty of saying "no" to the demands of children, the room all but quivered with excitement.

"They all say, 'I'm against it, I'm against it,' but they won't stand up and say so," said Mrs. Eunice Roediger.

"What are they afraid of?" I asked.

"They're afraid of being different," said Mrs. Morley Greis.

"My youngster said, 'Everybody can do it but me,'" said Mrs. Roediger.

"There is a wrong concept of values being developed," said Mrs. Royone Rauscher. "Later on they're not going to have that money. They're going to have a rude awakening."

"It's easier to say 'yes' than to fight your kids," said Mrs. Roediger.

"My children have no time just to think, to read," said Mrs. Jaquetta Bellman.

"Why don't you say no?" inquired Mrs. Greis.

"Because I've had it pounded into me that if they don't keep busy they'll be juvenile delinquents," said Mrs. Bellman.

The mothers and fathers then explored, without intervention by me, some of the causes that might be responsible for the obvious lack of brakes on the merry-go-round of their children's lives. Yes, they decided, the neighbors had something to do with it. Yes, and so did the teachers. And the various success-minded and promotion-conscious organizations that ensnare both youngsters and adults in Suburbia. But finally, Mrs. Roediger looked about somewhat defiantly and announced, "It's the parents who don't say 'no!'"

A chorus of agreement and relief went up all around the conference table.

In similar discussion groups elsewhere it was never too difficult to steer parents into recognizing, eventually, that when they talked in the third person plural ("They all do it," "They won't say 'no'"), the talkers were really talking about themselves. Let's listen in on a group of parents in Highland Park.

"There's too much tension, the kids are having too much to do," said an insurance executive's wife.

"Many of the kids are on a terrifically tight schedule," said another mother.

"Why?" I asked.

"It's conventional," said one of the fathers.

"My boy complains he only has Thursday afternoons with his friends," said a third mother.

"You can say 'no' to lipstick, but when it comes to a party it's awfully hard to say 'no' when all the children get invited," said a fourth mother.

"Why won't anybody break the pace?" I asked.

"We don't want to be squares," a father said with a wry smile.

A school administrator probed further into the lack of parental sales resistance against group pressures. "I think they're afraid their youngsters would rebel," he said. "In the past, 'no' meant something. Now I find myself asking myself about my own kids, 'What pressure will this put on my boy if the neighbor boy gets to go some place and he doesn't?' Then I find myself giving in when he asks a second or third time, and this is wrong!"

As everyone knows, kids are expert cajolers. Nothing makes them wheedle harder than the scent of weakness. If Mummy's sales resistance caved in yesterday on the matter of the week-end dance, isn't she likely to give in on the demand for a more generous allowance today? And if Mummy holds the line, why not put an armlock on Daddy? He is home so little that he might just possibly feel guilty enough to want to make up for his absence by shelling out some extra cash so Junior can have a good time on his own.

If they'll excel at nothing else later on, Suburbia's offspring will be artful lobbyists.

When I carried the discussions with parents further, and I attempted this only with individuals instead of groups, they usually got around to attributing their softness to their own childhood experiences. Today's

suburban parent is a depression child. He had it tough. He had to make his own way. He became a success, or else he probably wouldn't be in the suburbs now. Among the drives that spurred him on was the determination that his kids should have it better.

"I had to, but my Johnny isn't going to have to," one thoughtful father said. "I feel that way. I shouldn't, but I do."

Why shouldn't he feel that way? Well, this father said, his Johnny was having too much handed to him with too little effort. And why can't even this perceptive Daddy cut down on his handouts?

"I'm convinced that many parents can't say 'no' because they have identified themselves with their children," said a psychiatrist friend of mine with a sizable suburban practice. "It's like saying 'no' to themselves. The suburbs are places we would have liked to live in in our own childhood. I think it's the childhood dream gone wild."

So it doesn't too much matter how many parents realize that they are "spoiling" their kids or how many feel guilty about trotting along with the neighborly herd. The pressures we have examined are resisted by few because few want to resist them. So the majority lends almost automatic support to the suburban status quo as created by The Big They. After all, it isn't difficult to rationalize that the kids ought to "have fun," "do well," and "make the most of everything," especially now that they're among their "own kind" out in the suburbs.

By and large, I don't imagine that the resulting parental guilt feelings are likely to cause much psychic damage. I do believe that they heighten the suburban super-sensitivity to criticism.

We have run into a sample of these tender feelings in connection with the Highland Park reaction to the incident of the sixth grader who paid for his lunch with a $50 bill. *The Saturday Evening Post* article in which I reported this vignette unleashed remarkable vehemence on several counts. There were letters characterizing my reporting as "lies," "fantasy," "utter drivel," and so forth. At least one writer called me a "sadist" who evidently wants to herd Suburbia's little darlings back into the switchblade jungles of the decaying inner city.

Many reader reactions, especially the more thoughtful ones, adopted a defensive tone. Hadn't there been suburbs for as long as most of us can remember? If conditions are "terrible" in Suburbia, why haven't yesterday's suburban children gone to seed *en masse*? In particular, I enjoyed the note from the teen-aged newsboy in California who argued that I had libeled his trade because his parents were not driving him along his route regularly—just once in a while.

Interestingly enough, the reaction in Bellefontaine Neighbors differed markedly from that in Highland Park. There were few letters of protest from the Missouri community and none from informants who charged that I had "misquoted" them or "distorted" what they had told me. But there were many such accusations from Highland Park.

I can only guess why. My guess is that the lower-income families in Bellefontaine Neighbors, perhaps through their jobs and closer contacts with relatives and urban friends, are still maintaining a more realistic picture of the world; and, being realists, don't mind peering into a mirror and viewing themselves as they really are. Highland Park, on the other hand, is another step or two further removed from the non-suburban world; its aspirations and tensions run higher; so do its guilty feelings; and so does its sensitivity.

The soreness of Highland Park's toes revealed itself most clearly in the response to *The Post* article from teachers and others with whom I had talked, most of whom—unlike their Bellefontaine Neighbors colleagues—had not permitted the use of their names in the first place. *The Post* was hardly on the stands when some of these public servants sensed the outrage of their suburban customers and rushed into print in self-defense. Wyden was the curse word of the week.

"This man obviously came with ideas already formed and nothing we could say would convince him otherwise. In the article, he tells only half-truths." So wrote one school official in "Shoreline," the Highland Park High School newspaper. It so happened that this man had been among the most articulate, intelligent, and severe (if anonymous) critics of suburban child-rearing when I had talked to him. There were few sources from whom I learned more.

Another teacher, writing in "Shoreline," called some of my conclusions "inane and ridiculous." He wrote: "The reporter is also contradicting himself. He states that suburban children live in a vacuum, then goes on to state they have cars and money to travel. How can they live in a vacuum with these opportunities?" (As we have seen, this is easy for children who fly to Miami but are too privileged to grab a streetcar to go to a symphony concert downtown.)

Another of my most helpful informants, Mrs. Martha Winch, executive director of the Family Service of Highland Park, wrote "Shoreline": "I think that all of us felt bad about the impression that the article gave that Highland Park was somehow unique with respect to whatever aches and pains Suburbia was said to have. I would assume that these would prevail in any suburb that is similar to ours socio-economically and I would have welcomed a stronger spelling out of this [point] by the author."

The present report is, in part, an attempt to do so. I was also persuaded to tackle this effort because of the correspondence from all parts of the country that descended on me after *The Post* article was published. If I've given the impression that most of the mail contained stench bombs, let me correct it. The pros and cons were about evenly divided and both sides were equally emphatic. Some of the bouquets were touching. Here is one from a mother who is bringing up seven children in a Michigan suburb:

"I am looked upon as an 'odd-ball.' I am shunned and derided because we do not do as others do. Our children walk. Their idea of a Sunday afternoon is to walk the three miles to a local shopping center to browse. In the rain they walk, properly outfitted with hats and coats. I neither take them to school nor drive them home. They each have home chores to do. My boys can cook and clean as well as the girls (for this they are labelled 'kookies'). They are sternly punished for any and all infractions of the rules but are rewarded (simply, I assure you) for any and all jobs well done. As for grades in school, our attitude is not 'get good grades and see what you get.' Ours is, 'Get poor grades and see what you get.' The thing I am trying to ascertain is this . . . do you think that we are being old-fashioned? Are we raising our children in a manner which might damage them in any way? You have never seen a more uninhibited group of 'monsters' in your life. . . ."

I wrote this good lady that it didn't look to me as if she had much to worry about, but since the rest of her letter suggested that she was seriously worried and in need of reassurance that she was handling her children correctly, I looked up a well-recommended counseling agency in her area and referred her to it.

I wonder what happened to her at the agency. For,

difficult as it is to function as a nonconformist individual in Suburbia, it is far riskier yet for a publicly supported institution to stem the tide. Especially when it comes to criticizing the parents' jockeying for position on the achievement ladder which their sons and daughters must climb to insure the future of the next generation.

8. *The Great Expectations Syndrome*

The most subversive crime which a suburban child can commit is to be "average." Oh, the calamity of it! He's just *got* to be in the "top reading group." He's got to take extra "enrichment courses" after school hours or in the summer. He's got to go to a top college. He's got to excel, lead, push. Doesn't everybody?

Everybody certainly does—in Suburbia.

I used to think of this intellectual marathon in terms of great expectations. But it may well be that this is far too mild to describe the ambitions of many parents. "They're not expecting any more," a school superintendent said. "They're demanding."

Let's listen to the signs of ferment.

A grade-school principal said: "The mothers are always matching their children's grades. Everything is all right as long as somebody isn't pushing ahead of their child."

A teacher said: "The children all come and want to know: 'Which reading group am I in? Am I in the fastest?'"

A junior-high-school principal said: "Everybody in this community *has* to go to college—95 per cent or

98 per cent of them do, and some never should. One of our PTA board members told me his wife had their daughter apply to twenty-three colleges before the girl got in some place."

A friend of mine, a television producer, told me of a neighborhood boy who is none too bright but who would make a superb—and probably very happy—mechanic. Instead he is being pushed to go to engineering school. "He wouldn't dare not go to college," my friend said. "The reason why he doesn't want to be a mechanic is because he lives in. . . ." (and my friend named an upper middle-class suburb, where there are no mechanics in residence).

"Some parents are so anxious," said a high-school senior. "If their child doesn't reach a certain goal they push that child until that child is a wreck."

A nine-year-old, watching a TV commercial directed at parents who are planning to send their youngsters to "the college of their choice," piped up: "Mother, I think we better make our choice now!"

In a suburb of Washington, D.C., a couple of my acquaintance attended a meeting of parents whose children were about to start their freshman year in high school. "They all wanted their kids to get through in three years instead of four," the mother reported. "All the talk was about 'enrichment, enrichment, enrichment,' extra courses after school, extra courses in the summer."

"They were the intellectually greediest bunch of people I ever saw," said the father. "And everybody was exhibiting his kid. One father said, 'My child is fluent in French and Spanish, can't he just take Latin?'"

My friend's wife took up the account: "Finally, one mother got up and said, 'Doesn't this school have anything for children who're normal, who're just getting by?' At this point the Dean of Students got up and said, 'Why don't you people relax?'"

The parents who related this altogether typical incident were able to place the problem in perspective. They realized that IQs tend to run high among suburban parents. Naturally, they also run high among the children. But not all are equally endowed, and in Suburbia even the slightly less than bright come under pressure to be super-achievers.

"The so-called 'dumb' ones are plenty bright enough," my Washington friends said, "but they aren't being credited with it as they would be in a small town school or a big city school where the range is wider. Here, when a kid is just plain average, he's considered stupid."

Not many suburbanites are able to analyze the problem with such equanimity.

The Canadian team who studied "Crestwood Heights" concluded, "It is all too common to find in Crestwood Heights that many children are driven towards unrealistic goals. . . . Where the main preoccupation is child rearing, where the child is the focus of attention and the major concern of both the family and the community, it may well be that a child's failure to achieve is the greatest threat to family integration."

Dr. Dan W. Dodson, of New York University, reviewed similar surveys for the White House Conference on Children and Youth. The results, he reported, do not suggest "that all the pressures to achieve, or all the anxieties about college placement are in the suburbs, nor is it to say that other segments of the population do not also have 'great expectations' for their children. They do mean that when a class becomes segregated into homogeneous neighborhoods where roles must be validated by social class peers, the pressures are heightened and the concerns mount."

Plainly, we are back again to grapple with peculiarly suburban circumstances. Suburban parents tend to be bright, ambitious, hard-working, acquisitive. They've made their way by pushing ahead—else they probably wouldn't have landed in Suburbia. They're accustomed to competition and its prize, a measure of success. They want "only the best" for their children. And surely it has become a tenet of the American faith that every generation should be better educated than its predecessor.

New incentives are continually being added to fuel the big push. It is indeed becoming more difficult to squeeze children into the better colleges. It is also becoming more expensive, with the result that families with over-extended budgets must shove even their brightest kids harder than ever so they can compete for the ever more valuable scholarships. And isn't it true that fewer and fewer companies will hire—and fewer yet will promote—young executives who have somehow missed out on obtaining a college degree?

Not only is it un-suburban in the extreme to expect a child to march into the world without a white collar. It has also become unpatriotic. Mr. Khrushchev's Sputnik made life tougher for all American school children and, on the whole, deservedly so. But in the suburbs he has helped to raise even higher the educational sights of many parents whose goals for their children were already set too high.

Even in Bellefontaine Neighbors, 90 per cent of the high-school seniors go through school with some hope of going to college. The hopefuls included at least one boy in the 1960 class who had had serious difficulty making a passing grade in every one of his courses for the two previous years. Financial limitations make it impossible for most youngsters in this community to keep up in this respect with Highland Park or with Scarsdale, N.Y., where 95 per cent of the kids go to college, according to recent tabulations. Yet 41 per cent of the Bellefontaine Neighbors seniors do move on to higher education. Fully 12 per cent of those who start out drop out the first year because of scholastic problems. And every one of the drop-outs had been warned not to undertake the attempt.

Some youngsters who are pushed beyond their capacities become "wrecks" sooner or later. In Bellefontaine Neighbors one such boy committed rape and then killed himself. The more typical wrecking process was vividly explained to me by Mrs. Martha Winch of the Highland Park Family Service.

"You see, the dream is pretty big out here," she said. "Some fathers who are hard-driving executives set up pretty impossible standards. Some are quite intolerant of anything short of spectacular success. The achiever is more loved. Kids come in here who're perfectly all right, but they're identified as failures."

One characteristic case involved a father who had struggled hard to reach the top in his field. He had two sons. One boy did extraordinarily well. He was the father's pride. Every time the father looked at him he beamed. The boy was holding up the family prestige and satisfied the father's own deep need for his children to be successful. The other boy was not as bright, but his father demanded that he, too, become a top student. When the child could not satisfy his dad, the father withdrew his love. He looked at the boy's homework and shouted, "This is nonsense. Do it over." The more the father shouted, the less the boy could do. He felt that his entire family was ashamed of him.

A counselor discussed the problem with the father. Intellectually, he could accept that one of his sons was of average intelligence. Emotionally, he couldn't. He resented it and the child is now getting help from a psychiatrist.

Psychiatrists told me that children who are being pushed too harshly become some of their most frustrating cases. The roots of the parental demands are frequently buried in guilt or hostility feelings of the fathers. Some say to themselves, "Maybe I'm not spending as much time with the kids as I should, but at least I can get them to do well in school." Others say, "I worked for everything I got, by God, and my kid isn't going to come by everything so easy, either." The hostility sometimes leads to ridiculous punishments for poor grades. The penalties have been known to include withdrawal of allowances or TV privileges for periods of months.

"Sometimes I don't think it's as much an interest in the child as it's the hurt of the parent's pride," one psychiatrist said.

Under excessive pressure, most children function far worse than normally. They may be overcome by resignation ("I can't be as good as Dad or as good as he expects me to be"). Or they may be seized by fears working deeply into their subconscious ("I mustn't be as good as Dad or he'll destroy me").

Some children, deliberately or unconsciously, use academic failure as a weapon of retaliation against their parents. Just as young kids know they can revolt against their elders by refusing to eat, older ones quickly realize that they can strike back at their parents by flunking in school. There are many classic reasons why kids go into more or less open rebellion at various stages of adolescence. The "Great Expectations Syndrome" makes it easy to hurt the sources of authority.

Dr. Gustave Weinfeld, Highland Park's child psychiatrist, felt that the drive for children to be pushed more or less equally hard, regardless of abilities, is a pronounced suburban trait. "It's part of the parental set-up," he said, "the kind of car you own and what country club you belong to. It leads to dishonesty in children. I tell kids, 'I don't care how smart you are or how dumb, you're going to find some who're dumber and some who're smarter.'"

This is sound, relaxed psychiatry, but word of it does not appear to have circulated too much. As New York University's Dr. Dodson found:

"Not infrequently, parental concern leads to bribes, what some youths are calling 'academic payola,' to get the children to work harder in school. One New York suburb reported recently that several parents had offered their children a vacation 'on their own' in Florida at the semester break if they would work hard and achieve agreed-upon grades for the semester."

An isolated case? Not on your commuting life! A Highland Park high-school advisor told me: "Around here a report card with A's is worth so much; a touch-down is worth so much; the bribe is a big thing."

Dr. Dodson's assessment of this trend is not reassuring. "There is a growing concern for what this indicates about the values in such a society," he wrote. "It represents a seeking for grades as ends in themselves, or as status symbols, rather than a preoccupation with study for the sake of academic curiosity. It suggests a pressure from middle-class parents which strikes at the heart of more basic values."

The parents, as usual, have their defenses ready. We have already cited those extenuating circumstances which arise naturally from the suburban environment with its concentration of brains, hyper-active metabolisms, and sensitivity to "the times."

My group discussions with parents also permit the suspicion that many of Suburbia's mummies and daddies have become so engulfed in the pace and the competition that they have begun to see the kiddies as puppies yelping after a mechanical rabbit that is forever barely beyond reach.

"If the bait isn't held up, they're not going to snap," said a mother in one group, with the others nodding assent.

"You have to aim high enough," another lady chimed

in. "You have to aim higher than they're likely to go. Even if they're going to fail, you'd want them to try."

It is difficult for such parents to recognize that the unceasing chase after unattainable targets, the constant clambering onward and upward without pause (or too much concern for each child's individual limitations) can and does lead to maladjustments. Some people realize what's happening, of course. "Why does my boy have to be on top all the time?" asked a school principal and father. "Why *not* be a happy average? These people, when they're in a $10,000 house, they look at a $20,000 house. Pretty soon they're in a million-dollar house and still not happy. Why not be in the middle and be happy?"

Heresy, heresy, heresy. Its prevalence in the minds of quite a few school people helps to explain why parents strenuously challenge the right of school authorities to judge that their children may not be college material. Part of this resentment is reflected in an attitude of if-he's-so-smart-why-ain't-he-rich, which some ambitious parents bring to their encounters with teachers. But nothing ruffles a suburban parent's psyche more thoroughly than the results of testing programs, especially when they indicate that his child's intellectual growth potential lags behind parental expectations.

Reasonable doubts about the accuracy of projections which are often drawn from test results are certainly indicated. Maybe Johnny did have a cold the day he tackled his most important "battery" of multiple choices. How would Einstein have performed on the same tests? And aren't there plenty of cases of children who did poorly on tests in the lower grades only to blossom with scholastic brilliance when they entered college or even later in their careers?

Doubts and challenges of tests, though, are one thing. Cold fury is another. And fury, I'm impelled to report, is the only term adequate to deal with the over-reaction of some parents I've heard discourse on the subject. They radiate resentment of the school's authority and of reason itself.

"Every parent is ready to go over to the school and drop dead in front of some pea-brain just to get a kid into Harvard," began the explosion of one mother. "My boy's advisor says, 'Let's quit kidding each other; this boy is "C" material all the way through.' He's thirteen. Who are they to say this child's scholastic life should end because of one test? He was raised in an egghead atmosphere. Why should he marry a girl in a dime store? Will this make him happy? Who're they kidding? Let them educate our children and shut their mouths about testing. Don't make *me* feel as if I just got off the boat!"

The concern of school authorities and other specialists about the relentlessness of parental pushing is beginning to lead to some constructive action. It's high time. As long as parents exercise their taxpayers' rights in the running of their schools—and who has ever successfully underestimated the power of a suburban PTA woman?—they must be shown that what *seems* best for Johnny, sometimes isn't.

One of the best treatments I've read of the subject is a booklet called "Don't Push Me!" published by the Association for Childhood Education International (3615 Wisconsin Avenue Northwest, Washington 16, D.C.; 75 cents). It attempts, among other things, to clarify the difference between stimulating children and driving them. It even takes on the key argument of schedule-harried parents who correctly perceive that their children will lead an equally schedule-harried life and must therefore be prepared to live under pressure.

"No one is more used to being under pressure than the utterly defeated child," says one of the dissertations in "Don't Push Me!" "What children need is to be helped to respond constructively to pressure. They cannot do this if they are pushed beyond their depth, and they are not likely to do this if they *think* they are

beyond their depth. . . . It is not pressure put on children that is needed but better positive motivation. We find that the child who fails, the one in need of remedial help or the under-achiever, usually begins to find himself when the teacher helps him to find himself, when his parents accept him with warmth as he is. When this happens, he can see himself as someone of value, as someone with worthwhile interests and ideas, as someone who can do things. . . . Children today are in danger of losing the necessary growing years— growing years at children's pace—because of pressures to grow at adults' pace."

As the children grow older, there are inevitable over-reactions to the parents' over-reactions. A teen-aged boy, watching his father hound himself to death as executive vice-president of a bank, was asked what he'd like to be eventually.

"A ditch digger," said the boy.

We will have an opportunity later to speculate whether the banker's son will really wind up in the dumps. For the present I can only hope I've documented sufficiently that a good deal more hinges on the pressure to over-achieve than entry into a prestigious college or the choice of a career. And we're talking about more than an occasional lazy or unusually rebellious child, an occasional over-ambitious parent, or an occasional test result that might have been higher (or lower). We're talking about a new and greatly overcharged atmosphere for growing up. Nowhere is it more highly charged than in Suburbia. It's time to re-examine the intellectual hotfoot we're giving suburban kids before it singes too many of them too hard.

9. *The Button-Down Delinquents*

In the fall of 1960 the parents of Westchester County, New York, were presented with stunning news. In the course of an official investigation, 251 teen-agers and young adults confessed that they were narcotics users. Most came from socially prominent or at least well-to-do families and they were using marihuana and other narcotics largely at parties in their homes. For the most part, their parents would not believe what they were learning about their own children until they were confronted with incontrovertible evidence.

How common is marihuana smoking among Suburbia's young? Not very, of course. But then the use of narcotics is pretty serious business. Other forms of delinquency are more frequently reported in the suburbs. Stealing, for example. Or vandalism. Don't such excesses occur in all environments? Indeed they do. But the question needs to be asked why delinquency in any significant measure should trouble the suburbs at all. Isn't this one of the urban blights the suburban adults fled from? Wasn't Suburbia supposed to be the strife-free place purged of dirt, poverty, slum crowding, minorities, low-grade education, and all the other social problems known to be delinquency's breeding grounds?

It was. But as we have now repeatedly seen, the new environment has bred new problems. New—or newly aggravated—causes of delinquency are among these headaches.

Following the disclosures in Westchester County, *The New York Times* sought out several experts in search of the causes behind the criminal activities of youngsters who "have everything." A broad variety of explanations was offered. Escape from the "Dullsville" of emotional poverty amidst material plenty, for instance. Defiance of conformist parents. Attempts to bolster egos and gain group acceptance. Simple, if dramatic, reaction to affluence.

"We talk a lot about the things we give our kids," *The Times* was told by Alfred D. Buchmueller, executive director of the Child Study Association of America. "But the 'right' school and the 'right' clothes and the 'right' camp may not mean too much when they come from parents who do not give of themselves."

The man from *The Times* probed further. Sanford N. Sherman, associate executive director of the Jewish Family Service, told him that seeing parents sacrifice such human values as love and friendship on the altar of material success leads some children to become hedonistic. With downgraded standards and lessened controls, some children become impulse-ridden and seek to gratify impulses even if this brings them afoul of the law.

Eric D. Brown, director of psychiatric social services at Riverside Hospital, the country's only treatment and research center for drug users under the age of twenty-one, reported that many of its patients come from homes dominated by the mothers. And Sylvan S. Furman, executive director of the Manhattan Society for Mental Health, told the reporter: "Criminal behavior touches respectable parents to the quick. That's why children may unconsciously select this kind of behavior, rather than indulge in other disapproved practices."

My own travels bear out all of these observations, and then some. Let's stop first in the tiny, cluttered City Hall office of Michael F. Bonamarte, Sr., who comes from Flushing, Long Island, but has been on the Highland Park police force for thirty years. Most of that time he has been the department's juvenile officer. A small, wiry man with a graying crew cut and an uncynical smile, he enjoys the community's respect. I had heard his name mentioned frequently in previous conversations. People said they felt sorry for Mike. It must be tough, they said, to be a cop, priest, lost-and-found bureau, and Daddy-substitute to so many kids.

Mike agreed with them and said that it was getting tougher all the time.

Take the stealing.

"We had a boy here of thirteen from a very wealthy home," he said. "He steals a $47 toy train. What's a kid like this stealing for? Attention? For not getting enough love? Let the psychiatrist figure it out. Maybe it's because they have nothing else to do. They have everything. They steal books while they have money in their pockets to buy 'em. When I catch them they say, 'Everybody's doing it; why do you pick on me?'"

There is another kind of theft which is more of a suburban novelty. "We caught sixteen girls," Mike Bonamarte said. "They were stealing to keep up. They'd steal only the best $40 sweaters. We recovered about

$1200 worth. They just wanted to keep up with the other kids."

Bonamarte cares enough about his job to become considerably agitated as case after recent case flooded out of his memory. Almost invariably, the culprits came from the "best" families. There were the two high-school girls, aged fourteen and fifteen, who thought it would be sophisticated to become prostitutes. They sold themselves to eighteen boys in ten days at $1 per client. Then there were the kids who sold some of their clothes to raise money for the sessions of their poker clubs; the kids who lose wallets containing as much as $5 and don't even call to ask whether somebody found them; the sixteen-year-old who uses only distilled water to replace what he takes from his father's gin bottles because regular water gives the remaining gin an odd color.

Frankly, Mike felt sorry for his affluent taxpayer bosses, especially the fathers. "They really aren't head of the household any more," he said. "They come home and say, 'Boy, am I tired; let's have a drink.' The only time the family eats together is Sundays. I tell my wife at home, 'I hope we never get rich. People don't realize it. When they get rich they lose their family.'"

Bonamarte's counterpart in Bellefontaine Neighbors was less articulate but offered no conflicting evidence. She was Mrs. Loretta Voges, mother of a sixteen-year-old boy and juvenile officer for six years. She believed that parents let their kids get away with a lot because they are, quite simply, afraid of possible violent consequences if they try to enforce discipline. And, just as I heard again and again in reports of suburban delinquency all over the country, the kids in Bellefontaine Neighbors usually acted up just for the hell of it.

"Sometimes I work as a store detective in the Northlands shopping center," said Mrs. Voges. "It's really amazing what the kids take: clothes, records, costume jewelry, anything just to see if they can get away with it."

As to the causes peculiar to delinquent behavior beyond the city limits, lack of parental attention and control unquestionably leads the list. Teachers almost universally complained that they were frequently unable to locate either mothers or fathers in case of trouble. Some parents' ideas of "fun" are decidedly too advanced. One parent told me of once dropping in unexpectedly on a seventh-grade "slumber party." It turned out to be a co-educational party and the guests were dancing in their pajamas.

Again there is the elementary matter of parental example. Does the child lie and cheat? Well, maybe that's because he heard Daddy talk at dinner about a new gimmick to trick the government out of some income tax dollars; or because Mummy can be induced, from time to time, to compose a note to the teacher saying that Junior was indisposed when he really wasn't. Does the child lack respect for law? Well, maybe that's because he sees Daddy constantly exceed the speed limit. And in Highland Park there actually was a ninth grader who drove to Junior High School without a license. When the principal found out about it and wanted him to stop driving, the mother was quite exercised. The boy only used the car in the neighborhood, she said.

When it comes to the older children, Suburbia's lack of facilities is critical. At the seminar of psychiatrists which I mentioned earlier, the one sponsored by the National Institutes of Health and the Brookings Institution in Washington, several researchers hit hard at this want amid seeming plenty. "The most common complaint that you hear from the teen-ager is that there is nothing to do in the community," one of the doctors said. "And they are really right about that. There is the bowling alley and the movie house and whatever the school can provide; but there is no recreation center and the churches have very limited programs, if any."

Another doctor, who had conducted extensive studies in Levittown, N.Y., reported that its houses, as those in many other suburbs, are fine for families with small children only.

"The way the houses are constructed," he said, "they are boxes. The thickness of the ceilings means that when the kids upstairs are teen-agers, the house will be almost impossible to live in—I think one of the reasons the split levels are becoming more popular is that they sort of stretch the house out and allow a little more isolation. In Levittown, you don't have much of a (classic) class struggle, but you have a struggle between adults and teen-agers. The teen-agers, they're the real problem of Suburbia. . . . Whenever they want to do anything, the parents and police immediately expect it is negative. . . . When a boy talks to a girl, the parents immediately assume they are looking for a place to have sexual intercourse. There is a tremendous fear of anything the teen-agers do. And the teen-agers are very unhappy in Levittown. At the moment, they are a small minority, but when they become the dominant child group . . . I suspect all hell will break loose and the kids will have intercourse just to spite the parents. . . . They will tear things down just to spite the parents. . . ."

In all of this upheaval we have so far paid inadequate homage to the most potent instrument toward potential delinquency, the automobile. Not that it is merely, as one of my informants phrased it, "a motel on wheels." Far more significantly, it has become the decisive new symbol of independence and just-about-adulthood. And, as such, it falls into a teen-ager's hands relatively early in his maturity and, usually, without adequate preparation for the responsibilities involved.

If he was previously anchored too much to the immediate neighborhood and Mummy's availability as a chauffeur, he is now excessively liberated to pursue most any sport 100 miles away. If his associates were previously too rigidly homogeneous and parent-approved, they are now quite suddenly broadened to include just about anybody anywhere. If his opportunities to experiment were previously far too limited, they are now suddenly too unlimited.

Obviously, the cars are needed to make Suburbia function. And I know quite a few families where the use of automobiles is so regulated that they become useful tools in the parents' program to teach youngsters a sense of responsibility. But just as many suburbanites have yet to admit that the quietude of the subdivision may be deceptive, so they have yet to discover that you can't put a kid on wheels without causing him to roll—with just a touch on the starter button—into a world he doesn't really know much about.

10. The Anti-Coddlers

My older son was twelve and in the seventh grade when he launched a particularly energetic campaign for permission to stay up later at night. He wanted his bedtime pushed up to 9 P.M. His mother wanted taps blown at 8:30. The young man approached me on the matter and I advised him that his mother was, as usual, right.

"But Daddy!" came the wail, "it says right in the Parents Manual that 9 o'clock is the recommended bedtime for seventh graders. All the parents voted on it, don't you know?"

The young man had his facts straight. There was a Parents Manual. Nine o'clock was indeed the bedtime recommended by the suburban parents collective and I had heard that there had once been a vote on the proposition. However, I had not been aware that my son had studied the manual (shades of GI basic training!) quite so closely. Nor had I realized that his lobbying acumen had become sharpened to the point that he knew precisely when to attempt to pit the collective will of the other mummies and daddies against the will of his own parents.

Luckily, he had by then had considerable training in listening to a well-documented "no." Both from his mother and myself he gathered rather succinctly that (1) the Parents Manual was an interesting document; (2) other parents were perfectly at liberty to send their kids to bed at any time they pleased; (3) others were equally free to vote on any "recommended" bedtime they desired; (4) *our* children would go to bed when *we* told them; and (5) all other rules involving the upbringing of our kids would also be promulgated independent of the community's collective thought.

Our young lobbyist accepted the verdict without rebellion—that time.

Once more I would like to have the record show that my children do not have perfect parents. Nor was the case of the "recommended bedtime" a difficult one to adjudicate. As the children grow, so does the complexity of their problems and so does the relentlessness of community pressures on them and their elders. But the rub is that children won't accept standards unless they grow up with them from infancy. And suburban parents can't make the allowances necessary for a suburban upbringing unless they are willing to make one concession. To wit, they must concede that growing up in Suburbia, while delightful in many or even most respects, involves special problems which are, unfortunately, built into the newly constituted environment and into the psyches of the parents who congregate there and cause their energies, compulsions, and insecurities to fizz.

Most suburbanites I have talked to refuse to grant that special problems exist. Many who do recognize that there is something special about the suburban circumstances are inclined to shrug off the new problems as superficial ("So Miriam doesn't go see Daddy at the office; how often did I ever see my father at his office?").

The reluctance of parents to gaze at the realities is entirely understandable. Everybody in Suburbia is so busy. Then, too, it's really asking quite a lot to have the suburban converts find fault with a way of life that is so sanitary, well ordered, and expensive. Moreover, much of the disorientation of suburban kids is so clearly (and embarrassingly) traceable to the ways of suburban adults that the parents can hardly be blamed too much for preferring to change the subject when it comes up.

There are other excellent reasons why so many parents are so ardently on the defensive about their habitat. For some years now Suburbia has been important enough, sociologically speaking, to attract the attention of the type of researchers who swarm gleefully across the landscape armed with black-lens alarm-viewers. Almost invariably these scholars conclude that whatever menace they are currently studying will get us before the Neutron Bomb will.

Suburbanites don't mind being classified by scientists or pseudo-scientists. After all, that's the American Way. They do not, however, enjoy being classified as psychotics, alcoholics, and wife-swappers.

Interestingly, those who bristle most violently at criticisms of Suburbia generally fall into two very different categories. One is the cult of the closed mind. The other consists of the same people who do concede—at least in their heart of hearts—that all is not perfect in Faraway Acres. For mixed with the resentment of these good people is a solid dose of frustration. It is a frustration born of the knowledge that their children are growing up in an incomplete new world; that the kids are, to a considerable degree, prisoners of this world; that it requires enormous parental imagination, time, and effort to lower the bars in this most luxurious of jails; and that few parents, including probably themselves, will shoulder the attendant burdens.

Later on we will examine what can be done so the kids can hurdle the bars around their environment at least once in a while. Right here I'd like to point the finger at an exclusive group of suburbanites who have become particular heroes of mine. They are the resistance fighters, the anti-coddlers. They are Suburbia's conscience. Like all guerrillas they are boring from within—traditionally the most strategic location to bore from. They are unorganized and badly outnumbered, yet they tend to be stubborn. The most effective operators among this group manage to be formidable influences. All of them, like spacemen who know that their unearthly sojourns will be brief, are endowed with one characteristic of over-riding value to the people around them. That quality is perspective.

My travels convinced me that perspective is rare in Suburbia. I found it among some of the doctors, ministers, teachers, and other professionals whose views I have already cited. Exceedingly few parents were endowed with it. Mothers and fathers who do possess it, however, make themselves known easily (there are no inarticulate anti-coddlers in super-articulate Suburbia) and they are always a joy to discover.

I remember best, perhaps, a certain discussion with a small, informal assembly of PTA members. At the far end of the table sat an attractive young couple. In the early phases of the discussion they said little. Eventually the group got around to the omni-present problem that might be described as "Grass, grass everywhere, but not a place to play." All around the table the complaint was echoed that the area's collective standards for lawn cosmetics made it nearly impossible to assign the smaller kids places to romp without the closest supervision.

The young couple at the end of the table listened attentively. Finally the mother spoke up. She was experiencing no such difficulty, she said pleasantly. All faces turned in her direction. The lady flushed just a trifle and said, "We've just explained to the neighbors that we're growing kids instead of grass right now."

The chuckles around the table sounded slightly hollow.

I think they reflected incredulity more than anything else. Some day I hope to go back to this neighborhood and investigate what happened after the meeting. Probably not much did. Once a neighborhood collective has decided that lawns shall be maintained 99.4 per cent perfect, few householders will be plucky enough to become the obtrusive exceptions, thereby making themselves targets of the collective's gossip. It requires the perspective so rare in Suburbia to retain the notion that the purest function of a yard is to be the kids' roaming ground, not an idle adornment or testimony to perfect housekeeping.

Some of the anti-coddlers we have met in these pages are beginning to weaken. A case in point is that of the Michigan housewife who wrote me that she needed counsel because she was "shunned," "derided," and treated as an "odd ball" since her children had assigned chores around the house and walked to school and to the shopping center. Even a tough old cop like Mike Bonamarte feels he is losing ground. He objects to his thirteen-year-old daughter wearing falsies in her bathing suit. But her friends wear them and so he doesn't want her to be different and therefore unhappy.

"Usually I tell the kids to say, 'I got a tough old man; he makes me do this,'" Bonamarte said. "But how long can I take the pressure? What can you tell kids? I don't know."

Happily, some anti-coddlers who do know what to tell children are in good positions to make themselves felt. One of these is Dr. Weinfeld, the Highland Park child psychiatrist. Now sixty, he is a small, cheerful, agile citizen with close-cropped gray hair. He was born in Lima, Ohio, the son of a debonair and well-to-do cigar manufacturer. As a young man, "Gus" Weinfeld went into pediatrics. I asked him why. "Partly it was identification with little children, partly a desire to help children," he diagnosed.

Perspective on himself and his surroundings, the invaluable attribute of the suburban anti-coddler, came early to this doctor and it grew with his practice. Not too many years after he had settled in Highland Park back in 1930, Gus became troubled. "I could diagnose the rarest diseases, but I never saw them," he recalled. "I did see kids who couldn't eat and sleep. They had emotional problems. I just didn't know why kids didn't eat and sleep and had stomach-aches and I was terribly curious."

Gradually over the years, mostly after office hours, he acquired more and more training in psychiatry. He intended to use this knowledge only in his pediatric practice. But by 1950 the demands for his psychiatric services had increased so markedly that he completed the training for his second specialty and made it his exclusive concern.

Dr. Weinfeld is too canny an observer not to know the neuroses crackling all around him and he is too frank not to speak out on what disturbs him. To him the suburban difference lies mainly in the extreme intensity of the parents' struggle for status. He believes this to be the primary cause of such maladies as the pace of the Junior Rat Race and the blindness of parents to Suburbia's lacks. Parents complain to him about everything but the obvious. For example, he said, "I can't think of ever having had a parent say to me, 'Gee, I wish my child would go to a school that represents a better cross-section of people.'"

No doubt Dr. Weinfeld obtains a good psychiatrist's results with his little patients. But his field of operations is necessarily confined. He generally does not see youngsters until after they become seriously disturbed. By that time there is often not a great deal that can be done except for the doctor to become an understanding, yet non-coddling (and rather costly) father-substitute. Children who are not ready for the psychiatrist must have their anti-coddling administered at home or at school.

With notable exceptions, most of whom we have encountered by now, I found the school staffs allergic to conversation about the suburban difference. They know too well that they are, in effect, employees of the PTA—that most potent of the suburban collectives. PTA leaders generally look with disfavor on any eccentrics who attempt to rock the suburban boat. Most school people, therefore, follow the line of least resistance. As one seasoned Indiana-born school administrator put it, "We don't look on these folks as being different."

Those of his colleagues who hold a different view, for the most part, like to think of themselves as anonymous partisans skirmishing behind the enemy lines. But passive anti-coddling can yield only low-grade results. Anti-coddling is teaching. Teaching is explaining. Good explaining requires candor.

A man who knows this and daily risks the consequences is Arno Wehle, principal of Highland Park's Edgewood Junior High School, the fellow who popped off when one of his charges wanted to pay for lunch with a $50 bill. Athletic-looking at forty-five, this trim, open-faced principal wears a crew cut. Initially he is likely to register on visitors as a Mr. Bland, straight out of an Arrow collar ad. The impression could not be more deceiving.

Shortly after I first dropped in to meet Wehle, we happened to talk about the parents' chronic difficulty in restricting their children's television viewing. Wehle reported that quite a few mothers kept asking him what to do about this. He thought such problems should be coped with at home without outside counsel. But he had grown accustomed to this characteristic suburban extension of the teacher's role. I asked him what advice he issued to mothers about curbing the TV.

Wehle said, "I tell them that if the on-and-off switch doesn't work, there is always the plug in the wall."

His tone was chatty, but it did not lack authority. Anyone could have seen that he was not indulging in a flippancy. I know enough about Suburbia to realize, however, that not many principals could voice such common sense views in such plain language and still retain their jobs. Let us see how Wehle gained his self-assurance and why he kept his job.

Born and reared in Milwaukee, he was the son of a postal clerk. One of his early memories is of the time when he was eight and started visiting his grandmother by himself. Each trip required three different streetcars. On one of his journeys he lost his favorite Teddy Bear, but otherwise not much happened except that Arno learned to get around on his own.

His father considered travel an important adjunct of education and the family vacations were surprisingly ambitious for the time. Arno was still fairly small when the Wehles journeyed to Alaska and enjoyed moose steak. En route, as always, the father stopped at many post offices and talked shop. Later, back in town, Arno was occasionally permitted to watch postal operations from behind the counter.

While attending high school he worked summers as a dishwasher and assistant business manager at a YMCA camp. By the time he had gone on to Milwaukee State Teachers College he worked every night and all day Saturdays as a lifeguard and checker of gym suits at the downtown "Y." The clientele was not over-privileged.

"Most of the kids had baths only when they came to the gym," he recalled.

Wehle arrived in Highland Park in 1939, taught in the elementary grades, and became principal of Edgewood, then a brand-new school, in 1953. Meanwhile he had married his wife Gertrude, a fellow teacher who hailed from Oshkosh. The last time I visited the Wehles at their comfortable two-story frame house in Deerfield, a less privileged suburb adjoining Highland Park, their son Alan was seventeen and there was no sign of problems in the family that might have been induced by coddling or inadequate perspective.

Alan got an allowance of $8 a week. From this he paid for his lunches, transportation, haircuts, and entertainment. When he had permission to use the family car, he had to replace the approximate amount of gas he used. He took care of his own room and performed a number of definitely programed chores, including his mother's daily "small" shopping.

During the preceding two summers, while the family vacationed at their Wisconsin cabin, Alan worked in a nearby country grocery store as a stock clerk, unloading trucks and loading shelves. He also earned respectable sums as a caddy. ("He's so tight-fisted, I'll be out of money before he is," Arno said.) But when Alan and two buddies wanted to go to the cabin for three days of skiing in January, the Wehles decided that it would be too expensive to open the house and that the three boys ought not to be handed the responsibility of keeping house on their own.

On his job, Wehle believed in the same blend of reason, consistency, firmness, and explaining, explaining, explaining.

When Edgewood was first opened there were almost no officially proclaimed rules of conduct. Wehle told the students pointedly that there were, for instance, no rules against running in the hall or against chewing gum. He also told them that, if it became necessary, rules would be introduced.

"We've got a lot of rules now," he said. "The kids made it necessary. But I think I made them see the necessity."

Parents, Wehle said, are less inclined to accept the necessity for rulings: "The kids can accept an evaluation or a decision from the school; many of the parents can't."

Wehle has become adept at fighting off most attempts by parents to meddle in what is clearly school business. Some of the meddlers' complaints are remarkable. Once when Wehle's eighth graders were learning some of the intricacies of the graduated income tax, a father became incensed.

"Nine out of ten can't figure it out anyway," he said.

"To me, that's a very good reason for teaching it," said Wehle.

Nor is this principal reluctant to express himself on

those aspects of his students' private lives that affect performance in school. "Our kids are scheduled right to the teeth," he told me as he had told PTA groups. "If the parents were to take on the same schedules, they'd be dead."

It should come as no surprise that Wehle is frequently embroiled in controversies with individual parents and parent groups. He has won some battles and lost others. But he felt that he was getting desirable results. So did the parents. Throughout Highland Park Wehle's reputation was tops. It is not easy to buck a winning personality combined with competence and logic.

This is why Wehle kept his job at Edgewood Junior High School. It is also why other young suburbanites and their parents could be influenced by other anti-coddlers. There just aren't enough of them.

11. *When They Grow Up*

All right, then, what sort of grownups will the Subdivision Generation turn out to be?

Will their "filtered vision" and "horizontal experience" leave them permanently incapable of coming to terms with the world at large? Will their fathers' absenteeism turn the boys into emasculated neuters who can "bake a fine cake" but lack the essential attributes of manliness? Will the girls be bossy Amazons? Will their coddling mothers mold both sexes into a race of weak-kneed hypochondriacs? Will they wind up as naïve, frenetic snobs unable to face adult responsibilities? Will they stamp their feet and holler for Mama when they don't get their way in later life?

Nobody knows. Surely I don't. The emergence of Suburbia as a "dominant life style" is too new a phenomenon to permit conclusions. Nothing more than guesses will be possible for a good many years.

Personally, as I indicated at the outset of our excursions, I don't believe that the subdivision kids will turn out unhappier or more maladjusted than their forebears. With exceptions, my informants didn't think so either. Many of the most perceptive and critical observers I found appeared startled when I suggested that we might be rearing a new breed of faceless monsters. As soon as I asked them to peer into their crystal balls, the doleful conversations took a paradoxical turn and they predicted that the new suburban generation will turn out just fine, at least compared with its predecessors.

"They come through for you," said Arno Wehle.

"They have more sense than my generation did," said Highland Park's City Manager Ralph Snyder.

"They'll make us look silly," said a high-school principal.

These prophets might well be over-optimistic. My inquiries turned up sufficient evidence of conflicts and apparent deficiencies among the suburban young to leave a question about their general mental health. The scientific findings are extremely fragmentary. For the present they lean slightly toward the negative. Papers have been published in learned journals suggesting that there may be more emotionally disturbed children in the suburbs than elsewhere. The Canadian team which investigated "Crestwood Heights" concluded that the youngsters there were of "no better mental health, or perhaps worse" than kids in a sample of the general population of California. The Canadian suburbanites were given the same personality inventory tests as a group of young Californians hailing from a variety of backgrounds. The suburbanites performed insignificantly better in four of the tests, insignificantly worse in four others and notably worse in the remaining four.

No one claims that a few batteries of tests administered to a few children are bound to yield infallible guide lines. Nor is it impossible that the conflicts we have been discussing will produce some increase in the ranks of the nation's emotionally disturbed adults. But what about the vast well-scrubbed mass of potential graduates from the new Suburbia?

The experts admit that they don't know, but some are beginning to hoist warning signals. John R. Seeley, who headed the "Crestwood Heights" study, wrote: "The environment creates an excessively optimistic feeling as to opportunity. . . . The child's ignorance of conditions in which people live who are less successful than his father and his friends' fathers, furthers the illusion."

How injurious will the suburban illusion turn out to be?

Repeatedly I heard of adult apprehensions about "the tumble" from parental living standards which youngsters will be forced to take when they leave home and college and begin careers and families on their own. A Bellefontaine Neighbors minister complained: "These kids want to start out full grown. You should see the weddings we have, the flowers and fancy stuff—$100 and more just for pictures!"

More and more young married couples are being subsidized by their in-laws. This is leading to increased concern as to whether these new families would be able to weather illness, financial reverses, or other crises when they materialize. "What's going to happen to these kids when Dad isn't around to organize for them?" asked a teacher. "If we ever have a depression, we're going to have the biggest bunch of cry-babies you ever saw," said a mother.

Several social scientists with whom I talked believed that the new segregated upbringing will make kids from the big outlying suburbs much too class conscious. Nothing could be more logical. Already many adults have developed airs of superiority because of their new status as suburbanites. The best time to watch these feelings ferment is during annexation fights. Often the city's sewage and garbage collection services are too efficient and economical for an adjoining suburb to pass up. But almost invariably there is heartfelt sentiment that the suburbanites don't wish to have too much in common with the proletariat in town. In particular, they don't care to have their kids mix with "those city kids."

The suburban kids, as always, catch on quickly. They "know" that they are better than their city cousins. Their conversations were revealing. They said they got along better in the suburbs than in the city because "you're with people of the same class." When they discussed the relative advantages of city and suburb, they spoke of conditions on "both sides of the fence." One high-school senior said he wondered whether he was "prepared to live a lower-class life" after leaving home. A "disturbing" number of girls in the same school told teachers they would hesitate to marry beneath their parents' social status.

But there is another, brighter side to the suburban coin.

There is, to begin with, the natural resistance to damage enjoyed by children everywhere. "Kids can take an awful lot of trauma," a sociologist said. "I think most of us who have reared kids sometimes look back on our mistakes and wonder: how did the kids ever overcome them?"

Next we should remember that many distortions soaked up by the young suburbanites are temporary. Some misconceptions begin to fade when they embark on week-end or summer jobs. Other notions crack, as we have seen, when the youngsters become motorized. The military service shatters its share of illusions. So does the launching of a career. The "tumbles" to reality come late in life, but for the majority they do come eventually.

Most useful of all are, of course, the very real and important assets of the suburban environment. It shelters kids from much vital life experience, but it also protects them from the dirt, noise, and tensions of life among the switchblade knife set. It's gossipy, but all the jolly togetherness also spawns more community spirit and a feeling of more effective control over local institutions and public policies; the city runs its people, but people run their suburbs. At least they think they could if they cared to take the time.

Suburbia is bare of traditions and contrasts, but its newness generally lessens the influence of cliques and the conflicts between haves and have-nots; there is only the vast, galloping collective of the haves trying to amass new possessions at a roughly identical rate. Parental interest in kids may be too indirect or motivated by Mama's compulsion to keep up with Mrs. Jones, but the children feel and usually appreciate their elders' concern over the family welfare. The spirit of material and cerebral competition is certainly overdeveloped out there, but it also upgrades the quality of the schooling and community facilities.

There is general agreement that Suburbia endows kids with a maximum feeling of security, possibly because they like their environment so well. To them it is a near-utopia with plenty of elbow room, lots of friendly faces, unlimited hordes of like-minded playmates, and no major menaces.

Perhaps because they feel secure, suburban kids tend

to be tolerant. They lack understanding for the poor because poverty is simply a phenomenon beyond their horizon. But they are inclined to be kind to slow learners, to kids who stutter or struggle with other handicaps. The few Negro children who turn up in suburban classes are accepted and frequently more pampered than is good for them. They are victims of racial prejudice in reverse. A fourth grader who had one colored schoolmate complained to his mother: "Foster is all right, but he just expects everything! He's always first at bat and captain of everything!"

There is some question about the solidity of the suburban tolerance if and when subjected to stress. "Tolerance depends on whether you have a tolerable situation," said Robert J. Havighurst, professor of education at the University of Chicago. "Would these opinions stand up when the chips are down?"

A suburban psychiatrist asked a youngster what he thought of the possibility of going to school with a large number of Negro classmates, rather than the accustomed tiny minority.

"I'm scared," said the boy. The doctor called this a perfectly normal reaction to the unknown and pointed out that ultimately the suburban child faces an unusually large load of unknowns.

When I asked a high-school senior how he thought he and his friends might get along with a larger contingent of Negroes, he replied: "How can we say? We haven't been exposed to them. I don't see how we can form a real opinion."

It's this sort of perceptive reaction that makes you wonder whether some of the harshest criticism of suburban youth is a mere manifestation of each generation's conviction that the next one can't possibly be as capable. It certainly bears out the favorable judgments I kept hearing about the intelligence of the suburban young. Almost everywhere they were described as extraordinarily bright and poised, fast learners, and adaptable. Some teachers claimed that their charges knew perfectly well how over-privileged they are.

"They know all this isn't normal," said a principal.

Perhaps quite a few do. Their reactions to some of the suburban strains are encouraging. In Highland Park, some youngsters are deliberately escaping from the social whirl by starting friendships in neighboring Deerfield where the pace is less ambitious. And stealing, while not uncommon, is hardly the typical reaction to wealth. More likely, affluence gives kids a materialistic outlook that smacks of greed, but at the same time encourages them to cut loose from Mummy to rustle up some money of their own and thereby gain much-needed experience.

I, for one, also don't happen to believe that the bank official's son we met earlier, the boy who announced he wanted to be a ditch digger because his Dad worked so hard, will ever see the inside of many ditches. I bet he will become an executive and conceivably he will have learned a lesson from his father and subject himself to a less punishing pace.

Even the gloomy David Riesman concedes the existence of the hidden suburban asset which comes into view with such reactions of the young to their curiously tight, little world. In his introduction to "Crestwood Heights," he wrote: "One suspects that the maturity of the youngsters is in part the result of the conflict of cultures they must continuously reconcile at home and school."

I suspect, furthermore, that a certain amount of the tut-tutting about suburban youth is little more than a resentful farewell to another age, now gone for good.

Why should kids walk more when their elders don't and they themselves probably won't have to when they are grown? Could it be that much that is unprecedented and strange about the suburban upbringing is ideal preparation for the life most of the new generation will lead later, whether we like it or not?

The crowd instinct is strongly developed in them, to be sure, but doesn't modern life generally put a premium on gregariousness, on getting along in groups, on ability to toil in teams tackling complex problems cooperatively? Won't the talent for traveling in a herd come in handy too in the military and in many civilian occupations?

"I believe we're versatile enough to meet our environments," said a high-school senior. "We can conform."

Could it be that this talent will make him happier? Is it really desirable for many youngsters to look forward to anything less than life in a white shirt? Aren't the planners and the economists telling us that there are far fewer blue-collar jobs in our future?

Even the pace of the Junior Rat Race is not wholly without benefits. Isn't it likely that the time-consciousness instilled in suburban kids will enable them to roll right into the kind of time-budgeted routine that their fathers and mothers have been forced to adopt and that many of the youngsters expect to emulate to become "successful"? Will it make no difference whether the underprivileged remain distant curiosities to the kids if they're just boning up to be commuters anyway?

Reliable answers will be a long time in coming. The problems are too new; the future of our society is too uncertain.

What is certain is that there is indeed something special about suburban child-rearing; that the suburban experience is over-protective, over-simplified, and too lavish to insure adult stability in anything except an equally sheltered and prosperous setting; that a society stratified by income, religion, and race provides few opportunities to learn to get along with people who are "different"; that the narrowed, uniform horizons of the suburban "setup" will be no help in developing imaginative individuals required in a future society; that the conflict between the simultaneous pressures to excel and still to conform will confuse some youngsters, but will push others into finding their own way and thereby help them mature.

It is also beyond question that, whatever is lacking in Suburbia as a backdrop for the maturing of the young, not much is done about it.

12. *Meanwhile,*
Back at the Subdivision

Remember Streamwood, the look-alike, think-alike Instant Suburb near Elgin, Illinois, and how it was so neatly dissected by the YMCA? I talked to Dick MacMorran, the associate secretary for extension services of the Illinois area "Y" office, one of the supervisors of this canvassing operation. What was Streamwood doing about the problems of getting its children acquainted with the rest of the world?

MacMorran looked surprised.

"The people in this community don't feel they've got problems," he said. "They're pretty happy."

It's easy to see why the new, only-in-America formula for the deprivation of children isn't spotted by the Streamwooders. Suburbia's greatest sins are those of omission, not commission. Most parents don't recognize that the removal of grandparents from their children's environment, for example, creates a considerable void. To most adults it just means less in-law trouble. In actuality, this reaction is further proof of the suburbanite's abiding love for moving away from problems, from conflict. The result is to make it more difficult for the children to find roots and identity.

Suburbanites feel especially good about their surroundings if they are fairly recent escapees from Urbia. Suggest to them that the children are missing something in their costly new environment and these parents will study you rather closely. If you then still look reasonably sane and harmless to them, they will inquire whether they should perhaps move back to town to expose the kiddies to the decay which the family had just paid so dearly to shake off. What, they will ask, is so great about the modern metropolis? Isn't this cosmopolitan wonder turning more and more into a shabby island for the childless and the poor, plus a few enclaves for the very rich?

True enough, they can't go home again. Not, at least, as long as the children are living at home. But as the refugees' survival euphoria wears off, the children grow older, and "the setup" becomes more obviously preposterous, parents begin to cast about for ways to offset the new drawbacks.

Usually they have a chip on their shoulder about it. Ruth Millett, a syndicated columnist for the ladies' pages of the newspapers, voiced the prevailing sentiments like this:

"The big question is, what are we suburban parents supposed to do? Crowd back into the cities so that our children can have the broadening experience of playing in the streets, dodging switchblade knives and learning firsthand that everybody doesn't make as much money as daddy does? Or should our 'phantom fathers' give up their city jobs and their commuting and buy a little acreage in the country so that their children will have chores to do, will be toughened by walking miles to school and so that they can learn responsibility by working beside their fathers in the field?

"Obviously, we can't pick up and leave the suburbs—even if we wanted to, which most of us don't. So what's the use of trying to make us feel guilty about following the American dream of trying to give our children what parents naturally want for their children—a little bit easier life than they had, better educational opportunities, and a little more protection during their growing years?"

There, there, Miss Millett. Nobody suggests that you move back to Slum Square. No one wants your spouse to be a share cropper. And nobody is trying to rip the sprinkler system out of your little boy's school. Apparently, though, Miss M. is aware of at least some suburban excesses. She pleads for "just a little common sense" among suburbanites. This, she says, is all that's needed so "we suburban parents can have just as happy homes and bring up just as fine a generation of young people as parents anywhere have ever been able to do."

Agreed. But if my adventures permit just one generalization, I would say that common sense is exactly what Suburbia lacks most, at least in the matter of dealing with its offspring.

As we have observed, when the pressures become too much for the mummies and daddies, when it becomes tougher and tougher to say "No" and make it stick, the big thing now is for parents to get together in mutual protection associations and issue "codes" and "manuals" regulating the behavior of the children. I have studied some of these codes. They now exist for high-school as well as junior-high-school ages in at least a dozen states. They do not merely specify "recommended bedtimes";

they deal with dating, lipstick, driving, socializing ("party crashing is inexcusable"), and apparel.

I don't know how well these rules work ("The telephone belongs to the entire family and students' calls should be limited to five to ten minutes"). Naturally, most of the restrictions make good sense. Nevertheless, I confess to being appalled by the idea that it should require a social collective, no matter how benevolent, to tame my kid and yours.

No doubt some forms of group action are stimulating and worth while. I like particularly some discussion materials distributed by the program department of United Parents Associations, 44 West 28th Street, New York 1, N.Y. Here is a thought-provoking skit by Ernest Kinoy which is used by UPA to get parent groups to think and talk about some problems that really matter.

This drama is called "It Doesn't Grow on Trees." It's a bedtime conversation between a father, Ed, and a mother, Ann, about their daughter, Janey, and the doll she wants. The doll is a special new model. It is a "Hinds Honey and Almond" doll ("When you dip its hands in water, they get rough, red, and chapped. Then you put lotion on them and they get silky soft and romantically desirable"). The doll costs $12.95. Janey owns $7 which her mother borrowed to pay the cleaner. Janey wants the $7 back. She also wants another $5.95. . . .

ANN: Should I give it to her?

ED: For a twelve-dollar doll?

ANN: But Ellie Lou has one. I don't know how to explain it to her.

ED: Ellie Lou's Daddy has a Chrysler Imperial. Explain that to me!

ANN: I mean it. What can I say?

ED: Tell her . . . tell her it's too expensive! Tell her we can't spend that much money.

ANN: I did. She asked me how much your new tennis racket cost. . . .

ED: Seven dollars! Listen, when I was a kid we lived on seven dollars a week for food.

ANN: You didn't play with Ellie Lou.

ED: Look, I'm serious. I want the kids to have the best of everything, sure. But there's a limit . . . We've got a garage full of tricycles, bicycles, wagons. What are we raising? Gloria Vanderbilt?

ANN: You're the one who insisted on the English bike.

ED: I know, I know. I'm not saying it's you. It's both of us.

ANN: But you expect me to come up with the answer! Let's look at it from Janey's side. Seven dollars are hers. You know we've got $5.95 to spare. So does she. Then why shouldn't she have the doll?

ED: Because . . . because . . . it's too easy. What kind of an idea can she get of the world when everything falls in her lap? It . . . it destroys moral fiber, that's what it does! How is she going to learn the value of money?

ANN: She's a little young for economics.

ED: She's old enough. Let her get some idea that money doesn't grow on trees. We've got to find some way to teach her that life is hard, that it doesn't come easy, you know? That it's a struggle. Cold . . . cruel . . . harsh. . . .

ANN: We could lose her in the woods like Hansel and Gretel.

ED: We've spent seven years giving her a sense of

security. Maybe she needs a little insecurity. A kid has to learn that you can't take the world for granted.

ANN: The last time you decided to teach her that money didn't come easy for the family she went next door and explained her Daddy was very poor and borrowed a loaf of whole wheat bread. . . . She offered to work to earn the extra $5.95.

ED: Yeah? Where can she get a job? After all, what's she trained for?

ANN: She's serious. She told me Harry next door works regularly, and he's the same age. They have a schedule. He gets five cents for making his bed and five cents for minding the baby and a penny a night for putting his clothes in the hamper.

ED: That's fine. Do they pay him by the spoonful for eating? I don't see any reason why a kid can't be expected to help just because he's a member of the family. . . .

After considerable further discussion, Ed and Ann naturally decide to get Janey her doll ("We can call it a Thanksgiving Day present") and that's not all. As Ann put it, "You'll have to bring something for Tommy. We don't want him to feel rejected, do we?"

Unfortunately I have never had a chance to sit in on a discussion following the performance of this devastating yet constructive script. It does hold a faithful mirror before suburban audiences and no doubt some good comes of it. But only the individual application of individual perspective by individual parents to individual children can handle a problem such as saying "no" effectively.

Personally, I like to resort to kidding. My sons are constantly badgering their mother and me to do this and get that. Frequently their demands are not for something they want and expect, but something that has simply grown out of the community "pace" and been conditioned by the "setup." Frequently the answer must be "no." Frequently wails ensue. This is the time to be firm. By now the kids know that wailing is usually a waste of effort and they stop quickly. If they don't, I launch into a set commercial. It goes something like this:

"I know. You've got it very tough. Everybody gets to do everything. Only you don't. That's because you have a very bad father and a very bad mother. They don't love you. They don't give you anything. They abuse you horribly, etc., etc." Perhaps my boys have a perverted sense of humor. At any rate, they consider this spiel pretty funny, and it always shuts them up.

I have also taught myself to explain more of my own actions so the boys will appreciate their full context. When they first became interested in credit cards—and enchanted by the simplicity of this handy money-substitute—I kept pointing out that the use of these gadgets merely delayed the day of eventual reckoning and that paying for a month's gasoline is more painful than paying for a tankful at a time.

I still get questions about the cheating potential of my expense account:

"Couldn't you just take us along and let the office pay for it?"

"But that's stealing!"

This, I maintain, is talk that children understand and rarely question.

I have also collected methods devised by other parents to deal, at least partially, with such other problems as explaining fathers' absences on business trips. Some fathers make their trips interesting by taking out maps, showing the places to be visited, discussing the cities' claims to fame, and telling the youngster just what they will do in each place when they get there. One mother made a calendar for her three-year-old with a different colored strip of paper representing each day her Daddy would be away so that the child could tell by herself when he would come back. Occasionally, fathers find it possible to take their children on business trips and let them tag along as they transact their business. Quite a few mothers hoard evidence of their children's accomplishments in school and home for "Daddy when he comes back." I try to write my boys at least briefly each day when I am away and tell them something of what I have been doing.

There is no need to create artificial chores to instill a sense of responsibility in youngsters. Plenty remains to be done around any household. Beds are still made—and dinner tables set—without push buttons. Children can be taught to be helpful—and without being paid for it. They can be encouraged not only to accept outside jobs, but to take them seriously, not to undertake anything they don't intend to do competently and to finish.

They can be taught that the herd's way is not necessarily the only way. They can be taught to question, to stand up and be counted. At a workshop conducted by the National Conference of Christians and Jews, parents were advised: "Allow him to be himself at home, and he will allow for differences away from home. He will be able to accept others, whether or not they are like he is."

On the other hand, I think it is important not to

preach too much and, if possible, not to be too dull and abstract. A good story often helps drive home a timely point. My older boy had barely entered junior high school when he delivered himself of a detailed diatribe against certain of his teachers. To hear him tell it, these ladies were demons who breakfasted regularly on fried children. I asked him where he had acquired his knowledge. "Everybody," he said, had told him. The horrible facts were well known to his cronies, and he proceeded to enumerate the usual list of his informants. I talked to him briefly about the unfairness of making snap judgments, especially about other people, and then told him about the late Senator Joseph R. McCarthy, the smear tactics of McCarthyism and how they became discredited. The young man, like most, is interested in history, especially of the violent kind. He was fascinated by the McCarthy story. And he understood its connection with his own unsubstantiated views about his teachers.

Once parents recognize more candidly what Suburbia lacks, they will find plenty of opportunities to tell their kids about differences between the suburbs and the rest of the world, and they will then be more ready to go to the (often considerable) trouble of demonstrating these differences in the flesh.

They can invite foreign students to their homes. They can take better advantage of their children's teeming curiosity, keep up contacts with relatives and friends in older neighborhoods or on farms, and not restrict family vacations entirely to the "good" resorts. They can plan more imaginative excursions to city schools, restaurants, museums, and other institutions.

It is not useful, however, to make too much of a

"project" out of adventures away from the home setting ("This is the day when we'll go see how Negroes
live"). Kids tire notoriously fast in museums; and suburban schools have found exchange visits with schools
in underprivileged neighborhoods not excessively pro-
ductive—even when they lead, as they sometimes do, to
"pen pal" friendships with youngsters who live in the
same city, yet literally a world away.

"These things turn into sideshows," one teacher said.

The best way to teach children to broaden their horizons is for parents themselves to live with, and enjoy,
broad interests. Children read most in homes where
parents read. Children become interested in news of
politics and culture when they notice that their parents
are involved in such interests. Juvenile social life can
be de-emphasized by some co-operation among parents and by keeping down costs. A more realistic concept of money can be taught by detailed comparisons
with incomes and habits of the less affluent.

Above all, kids can be taught to be more critical.
"Let them learn you don't have to accept everything,"
said a psychiatrist. "Let them look at things all around
us and see that there are alternatives."

As suburbs become bigger, farther removed from
the city, and apparently more self-sufficient, the con-
scientious parents' job will become more difficult. Some
experts think the answer is to make the suburbs even
more self-contained. "I don't think you can teach everybody to boil water," said one planner. "We put in water
supply systems so you don't have to boil it." But others
doubt that Suburbia and its ruling mentality will lend
itself to the installation of adequate "systems" to supply
reality. They believe that better appreciation between

suburb and city is the answer—and such a mutual appreciation society is not in sight.

The White House Conference on Children and Youth heard this from its briefers:

"It seems singular that with all of our development of communications, the 'togetherness' of family life, the return to the church, and group emphasis in education and living, we are becoming increasingly aware of a sense of alienation in the metropolitan man's innermost psyche. May this not be the inevitable consequence of life 'sealed off' into socio-economic and racial ghettos? In the inner city today is left one of the few places in America where man can still make outreach to his fellow man across lines of race, nationality or creed. Symbolically the inner city represents the whole—mainstream in a unique sense. One cannot leave it without sensing that he is leaving the 'center of things.' These heterogeneous populations represent for us all the 'stranger' with whom we must come to grips if we are to validate our sense of selfhood with the broad stream of human kind.

"Whatever our protestations of faith and democratic ideals, our children learn what they are living. The suburb teaches not what we say, but what our behaviors indicate. How to preserve the advantages of the suburb and recapture our sense of community with the total metropolis is perhaps our greatest task ahead."

P.S.

We have made the rounds, heard the voices, and seen the sights. I'd like now to include another small service in the price of this report.

Whenever I have spent extended periods trying to fathom something new and involved and then writing about it, readers who maintain that they have thoughtfully perused the fruits of this endeavor have liked to take me aside, snub out their cigarettes firmly, and demand, "All right now, just between us, what do you *really* think?"

All right, I'll tell you what I really think.

I don't know about your kids, but I think mine will be pretty much OK. I suspect they'll be ambitious and efficient, and they won't smoke cigars and become journalists because I've warned them graphically enough about the dangers of both of these pitfalls. I think they —and the rest of the Subdivision Generation—will have their troubles. Many of their troubles will be brand-new, nifty ones that we haven't even thought about yet. But some of the potential after-effects of their peaceful suburban upbringing are preventable, like hangovers. I'm therefore attempting to do whatever I can to soften the edges of my boys' eventual hangovers. Because they're really rather nice kids.